A CASEBOOK

FOR

AIR TRANSPORTATION

A CASEBOOK FOR AIR TRANSPORTATION

Alexander T. Wells
Broward Community College

Wadsworth Publishing Company
Belmont, California
A Division of Wadsworth, Inc.

Aviation Education Editor: Anne Scanlan-Rohrer
Editorial Assistant: Leslie With
Production: Ruth Cottrell
Print Buyer: Randy Hurst
Designer: Cynthia Bassett
Copy Editor: Sheryl Rose
Compositor: David Woods
Cover Photo: George Hall/Check Six
Signing Representative: John Anderson

Printed in the United States of America

1 2 3 4 5 6 7 8 9 10 — 94 93 92 91 90

Library of Congress Cataloging in Publication Data

Wells, Alexander T.
A casebook for air transportation

1. Aeronautics, Commercial—Management—Case studies.
2. Airlines—Management—Case studies. I. Title

HE9781.W453 1989 387.7`068 89-24759

ISBN 0-534-12534-4

CONTENTS

PREFACE

This casebook was designed for air transportation courses to supplement and complement the material covered with practical applications. Although names and statistics are hypothetical, the cases illustrate actual company situations and management decision-making processes drawn from the experiences of real mangers.

The cases selected are representative of the vital decisions that influence the overall competitiveness of the firms under analysis. Even though ten years have passed since airline deregulation became a reality, U.S. airlines still remain in transition from a highly regulated economic environment to one that is much less regulated. Deregulation has had the effect of spurring competition and providing more price-service options. Passenger traffic has more than doubled, causing serious airport/airway congestion and delay problems. These problems have been exacerbated by scheduling practices flowing from deregulation, including increased emphasis on hub-and-spoke scheduling. There has been a high mortality rate for new entrants and after some initial problems of adjusting to the new environment, the largest carriers have displayed a more powerful market presence in recent years. Merger activity has increased significantly and there is some speculation that the industry may shake down to a comparatively small number of large, strong survivors supplemented by smaller regional carriers.

Unquestionably, the deregulation environment has lowered labor costs and generally intensified pressure on management to operate more efficiently. Yet, for various aspects of operations, deregulation has unavoidably reduced efficiency. This includes fleet planning trends where postderegulation market fragmentation has led to smaller planes, forgoing the seat-mile cost efficiency of large aircraft.

The intensified competition resulting from deregulation has accelerated changes in airline marketing strategies and techniques, particularly those aimed at the higher-paying business traveler. Mileage bonus plans have proliferated and have become a means of buying the brand loyalty of frequent flyers by providing future free trips as the reward to accumulating trip mileage on a specific airline. The marketing power of travel agents has become greater under deregulation, partly because of the greater complexity of fare and schedule options and the increased reliance on agents to find the most favorable choices for a given itinerary.

The air transportation industry has not reached an equilibrium point, and there remains much uncertainty and misunderstanding over the deregulatory impacts being experienced. Within this economic milieu the cases in this book take place. Basically, the cases present an inside look at the industry through situational analysis rather than the more conventional theoretic construct approach taken in textbooks. Each case gives a situation and the views of the management, but the final analysis and conclusion is up to the student. As in the real world, students must first define the problem, determine the most important facts relating to the problem, analyze the facts, come up with alternatives, and finally make a recommendation to management. The questions following each case are not intended to direct the discussion. They are there to help students analyze the case in advance and prepare for the discussion. By working through the case studies presented here it is possible to derive general principles of good management. This is done by treating the casebook as a unit, considering all the case studies together. The principle is that good decisions relating to one area within a company can apply to other areas of the firm. The primary purpose is to teach the elements of industry analysis and, so far as is feasible, to place students in the industry environment so that they can draw on their own knowledge and stimulate the decision-making process that might be expressed in the environment. Students should not look for one "right" answer to a case problem. They should look for all possible alternatives from which to select the one—or several—most likely to succeed under existing conditions.

This casebook can be used as a supplement to my text, *Air Transportation: A Management Perspective*, Second Edition (Wadsworth, 1989), or can be used as the core text for applications-oriented air transportation courses.

ACKNOWLEDGMENTS

This casebook bears the imprint of many professors and company officials who developed or contributed material which in some form has found its way in to this book and the Instructor's Guide to accompany it. A book of this sort must capsulize existing knowledge while bringing new perspectives and organization to enhance it.

Over the years I have used many cases published by Harvard Business School in my aviation management courses. I have found these cases to be very current and comprehensive and highly recommend their use in upper level courses. Although the cases appearing in this book were developed by me, I would be remiss if I did not thank Harvard Business School for the many concepts, approaches, and situations that I learned by using their material and subsequently adapting it to fit my cases. My thinking and the cases herein have been shaped by the writings of many scholars and practitioners. I gratefully acknowledge their contributions.

Finally, I would like to thank the following reviewers: John L. Carkeet, Florida Institute of Technology; Gerald Fairbairn, Daniel Webster College; Dan Hejde, Parks College of St. Louis University; and David A. NewMyer, Southern Illinois University at Carbondale.

A CASEBOOK
FOR
AIR TRANSPORTATION

Introduction
Methods for Developing Fare Comparisons for Exhibit 1–1
Factors Contributing to Fare Variation

1
DOMESTIC AIRLINE PRICING UNDER DEREGULATION

INTRODUCTION

The widely held public impression is that deregulation has lowered airline fares. However, that impression is only partially valid. The fact is that deregulated fares are lower on some routes but higher on others. Fares have been in a continuing state of change since deregulation, often varying dramatically from one date to the next for the same trip. On some routes, fares have been reduced by deregulation to levels below those of 1978 but on other routes fares have doubled—or more than doubled—in this same period. This case discusses airline pricing and examines the trends of industry aggregate pricing data and variations within those data.

METHODS FOR DEVELOPING FARE COMPARISONS FOR EXHIBIT 1-1

Exhibit 1-1 depicts a sampling analysis of the fare variations among domestic routes. Because of the enormous variation in (and volatility of) airline pricing in recent years, a comparison of fares cannot present a complete picture of the pricing "universe." All that can be done in relation to this constantly changing scene is to present what amounts to a "tip-of-the-iceberg" snapshot of a sample of the variation as it existed at one instant of time.

In drawing the sample for this snapshot, care was taken to establish sampling rules that would assure absence of bias in the selection of city pairs to be reviewed.

Once the city pair sample was drawn by these rules, the fare reference section of the April 1984 Official Airline Guide (OAG) was used to determine the lowest "effectively available" one-way coach fare. Then the April 1978 OAG was used to determine the most nearly comparable fare available in that past period. These dates were selected because they represented a period before deregulation and before the sunset of the CAB.

Procedure for Obtaining Random Sample of City Pairs

It was deemed important to obtain a city pair sample that would provide a cross section of markets of different stage lengths and different traffic densities. The procedure employed was as follows:

1. A list of "base cities" was drawn from Table 3 of the CAB Origination & Destination (O & D) Report (Table 3 ranks all cities in terms of their total O & D passenger volume). Using this table, the base cities taken were those ranked 1, 11, 21, 31, and so on. A total of seven such base cities was drawn.

EXHIBIT 1–1 Comparison of One-Way Coach Fares between Specified City Pairs

City Pairs	Distance (Miles)	Lowest Effective One-Way Fare 4/78	Lowest Effective One-Way Fare 4/84	% Chg 1978/1984	Lowest Effective One-Way Fare Curr Yr	%Chg 1978/Curr Yr	Fare per Mile 4/78	Fare per Mile 4/84	Fare per Mile Curr Yr
1. Syracuse-Albany	119	$34	$50*	+ 47 %			29 ¢	42 ¢	
2. New York-Albany	136	32	67*	+ 109			24	49	
3. New York-Binghamton	146	39	86	+ 121			27	59	
4. Salt Lake City-Pocatello	150	33	64	+ 94			22	43	
5. Nashville-Birmingham	177	36	101	+ 181			20	57	
6. Syracuse-New York	197	38	38	—			19	19	
7. Miami-Tampa	205	38	44*	+ 16			19	22	
8. Nashville-Atlanta	214	40	119	+ 198			19	56	
9. Syracuse-Philadelphia	228	41	116	+ 183			18	51	
10. St. Louis-Kansas City	237	42	59*	+ 41			18	25	
11. Miami-Daytona Beach	239	51	59*	+ 16			21	25	
12. St. Louis-Chicago	258	44	79*	+ 80			17	31	
13. Syracuse-Boston	264	54	98*	+ 82			21	37	
14. New York-Portland (ME)	269	46	38	-17			17	14	
15. New York-Norfolk	296	47	38	-19			16	13	
16. St. Louis-Cincinnati	307	49	162	+ 231			16	53	
17. Columbus (OH)-Washington	321	49	70	+ 43			15	22	
18. Nashville-Charlotte	328	53	107*	+ 102			16	33	
19. Columbus (OH)-Nashville	337	75	175	+ 133			22	52	
20. Salt Lake City-Denver	380	56	70	+ 25			15	18	
21. St. Louis-Chattanooga	383	56	188	+ 236			15	49	
22. Salt Lake City-Billings	387	57	168	+ 195			15	43	
23. Miami-Tallahassee	403	58	108*	+ 86			14	27	
24. Columbus (OH)-Philadelphia	404	59	149	+ 153			15	37	
25. Syracuse-Norfolk	429	61	60	-2			14	14	
26. New York-Jacksonville (NC)	458	77	149	+ 94			17	33	
27. New York-Columbus (OH)	476	65	60	-8			14	13	
28. Miami-Charleston (SC)	491	75	168	+ 124			15	34	
29. Salt Lake City-Albuquerque	492	84	181	+ 116			17	37	
30. Salt Lake City-Phoenix	507	74	129*	+ 74			15	25	
31. St. Louis-Dallas	550	72	139*	+ 93			13	25	
32. Salt Lake City-Los Angeles	590	74	200	+ 170			13	34	
33. Nashville-Omaha	611	77	156*	+ 103			13	26	
34. St. Louis-Columbia (SC)	612	80	223	+ 179			13	36	
35. New York-Augusta (GA)	678	81	204	+ 152			12	30	
36. Nashville-Allentown	683	82	215	+ 162			12	32	
37. Columbus (OH)-Omaha	687	84	236	+ 181			12	34	
38. Nashville-New York	762	88	169*	+ 92			12	22	
39. Syracuse-Atlanta	793	90	255	+ 183			11	32	
40. St. Louis-Philadelphia	810	92	135*	+ 47			11	17	
41. Salt Lake City-Oklahoma City	863	115	125*	+ 9			13	15	
42. Columbus (OH)-Oklahoma City	863	100	249	+ 149			12	29	
43. St. Louis-West Palm Beach	1023	108	185*	+ 71			11	18	
44. New York-West Palm Beach	1036	108	99	-8			10	10	
45. Miami-Cleveland	1082	112	139*	+ 24			10	13	
46. Nashville-Albuquerque	1119	122	238*	+ 95			11	21	
47. Miami-Hartford	1196	120	304	+ 153			10	25	
48. Miami-Boston	1259	125	149*	+ 19			10	12	
49. New York-Oklahoma City	1337	132	199*	+ 51			10	15	
50. Columbus (OH)-Albuquerque	1339	132	321	+ 143			10	24	
51. Miami-Bangor	1460	140	339	+ 142			10	23	

* Capacity control restrictions apply.

EXHIBIT 1–1 (continued)

City Pairs	Distance (Miles)	Lowest Effective One-Way Fare 4/78	4/84	% Chg 1978/ 1984	Lowest Effective One-Way Fare Curr Yr	%Chg 1978/ Curr Yr	Fare per Mile 4/78	4/84	Curr Yr
52. St. Louis-San Diego	1553	148	159*	+ 7 %			10 ¢	10 ¢	
53. New York-Amarillo	1555	148	350	+ 137			10	23	
54. St. Louis-Reno	1569	157	350	+ 123			10	22	
55. Salt Lake City-Atlanta	1583	153	353	+ 131			10	22	
56. St. Louis-Los Angeles	1588	149	350	+ 135			9	22	
57. Miami-Denver	1714	160	209*	+ 31			9	12	
58. St. Louis-San Francisco	1730	160	360*	+ 125			9	21	
59. Nashville-Ontario	1746	164	324*	+ 98			9	19	
60. New York-Albuquerque	1815	167	204*	+ 22			9	11	
61. Salt Lake City-New York	1975	179	195	+ 9			9	10	
62. Salt Lake City-Hartford	2019	182	420	+ 131			9	21	
63. Columbus (OH)-Portland (OR)	2028	183	373	+ 104			9	18	
64. Syracuse-Phoenix	2040	184	385	+ 109			9	19	
65. New York-Phoenix	2142	191	325*	+ 70			9	15	
66. Miami-Ontario	2291	204	283	+ 39			9	12	
67. Syracuse-Los Angeles	2344	205	403	+ 97			9	17	
68. New York-Ontario	2417	213	433	+ 103			9	18	
69. Miami-San Francisco	2579	223	318*	+ 43			9	12	
70. Miami-Portland	2695	232	309*	+ 33			9	12	

* Capacity control restrictions apply.

2. A matrix was then developed for each of the seven base cities, seeking a sample of city pairs linked to those base cities, with the cells of the matrix providing a cross-classification of varying mileage blocks and traffic density blocks. Specifically, three mileage categories were used (0 to 400 miles; 401 to 1,500 miles; and more than 1,500 miles). Four traffic density categories were used (10 to 50 O & D passengers per day; 51 to 200 passengers; 201 to 500 passengers; and more than 500 passengers).

3. Beginning at rotating alphabetical starting points within Table 8 of the O & D Report for each of the base cities, city pairs involving those base cities were placed in the appropriate cross-classification cells of the above-described matrix until each cell had a maximum of three city pairs. (Except for the largest base cities, not all cells could be filled with three city pairs each, simply because the smaller base cities did not have that many city pairs meeting the twofold criteria of mileage/density.) The sample drawn by this methodology provided 70 city pairs.

Ground Rules for Fare Determination

The objective was to obtain fares that were the lowest "effectively available" on a one-way basis. The term "effectively available" meant that the average passenger would have a reasonable chance of getting access to this fare. It would not have been meaningful to have included low fares available only on a very limited basis by a carrier offering virtually no service in a given market. At the other extreme, it would also have been misleading to limit the fares only to those offered by the largest carriers in the market. To avoid either form of distortion, a fare was treated as effectively available if it was offered by a carrier that had a significant (though not necessarily dominant) presence in the market. (For example, in any market served by People Express, that carrier's fare was treated as the lowest effectively available fare, regardless of whether most or all of the other carriers on the route matched it.)

When a "capacity controlled" fare was published for one-way effectiveness, that fare was used even though there was no way of knowing the degree of limit placed on the number of seats available at this fare.

To validate the representative nature of the fare data obtained by these rules from the OAG source, spot checks were made by telephone calls directly to the reservations offices of the several airlines. This was done where the data indicated an especially high inflation in the fare since 1978. The spot check phone calls confirmed the data as being accurate.

In both periods, there were some lower fares available that required advance booking, round-trip travel, and minimum trip duration. Since such conditions automatically excluded much of the market, it was felt that the most meaningful comparison would be in terms of fares that could be bought without advance arrangements and on a one-way basis.

The "lowest effective" fare this analysis sought to show is the fare that would actually be found by a substantial portion of passengers traveling on the given route. In some of these markets there were other, lower fares available on carriers who were minor participants in the market (for example, some special low fares available only on connecting schedules in markets where the bulk of the traffic moves on nonstop flights). To show such a special fare as the going rate for the given market would give a misleading picture, since so few passengers on the route would actually get this fare. Therefore, this analysis deals only with fares offered by carriers deemed to be significant participants in the market.

The pricing disparities indicated in Exhibit 1-1 do not represent some temporary aberration. The April 1984 period covered by this analysis was not one of extraordinary fare-war activity. In other periods (such as early 1983) the disparities would have been even greater. Fare disparity has become an on-going phenomenon of deregulation. For example, a traveler flying between St. Louis and Chattanooga paid 49 cents per mile in 1984 (#21), while another flying virtually the same distance between Salt Lake City and Denver (#20) paid 18 cents a mile.

FACTORS CONTRIBUTING TO FARE VARIATION

The significant variation in fares indicated in Exhibit 1-1 can be understood only by first considering the nature of airline costs and competitive pressure as they affect individual market fares.

In its final report to Congress the CAB stated, "Fare differences between markets are now more likely to be the result of cost differences." However, this has never been supported by published analyses considering in detail the significant fare variations between individual markets, or indicating how much of the pricing disparity could be specifically correlated with identifiable cost variances. The very concept of airline costs is a fluid and flexible one, creating a wide spectrum of costs within which individual airlines can rationalize their market fares. In practice, it is the varying intensity of competition that determines where within the broad spectrum of "costs" the precise fare will be established.

At one extreme, when a carrier is considering how to price an otherwise empty seat on a schedule that is already committed to be flown, the marginal cost of filling that empty seat is very close to zero. The basic cost of fuel, crew pay, landing fees, depreciation, and maintenance will not be affected by whether there are 101 passengers instead of 100 on a B-727. Thus, airlines usually view the "empty seat" marginal cost as almost nil and regard almost any token revenue as preferable to the zero revenue from an empty seat.

At the next plateau of cost recovery is the variable cost of flying the plane (that is, the cash out-of-pocket operating costs, excluding fixed and overhead system costs). In the short run, fixed and overhead costs are not likely to be affected by whether or not a given schedule or route is operated, and consequently pricing that is related only to variable operating costs is sometimes acceptable, particularly where a more stringent cost test would result in grounding the plane and underutilizing other resources.

Finally, the "fully allocated" cost basis for pricing is the one level of pricing that seeks full recovery of all costs, fixed as well as variable.

Prior to 1978, with regulation of fares, the CAB attempted to take all cost variables into account, disallowing those that appeared to reflect operational inefficiency. The CAB then averaged the allowable costs into one overall formula. This represented a consolidated industry cost level, intended to reflect efficient operation under existing technology. The formula was intended (in its average system impact) to cover fully allocated costs, including a fair return on investment subject only to the exclusion of those costs specifically found by the CAB to represent inefficient management.

The CAB formula recognized that costs vary inversely with segment length; therefore, the formula included a taper so that fare per mile sloped downward with increasing distance. (The specific CAB formula as it existed for January 1, 1983, was: coach fare = $27.68 plus 15.14¢ for all miles up to 500; plus 11.55¢ for miles between 501 and 1,500; plus 11.10¢ for all miles beyond 1,500.)

In setting this formula, the CAB acknowledged that there were many aspects of cost variation besides mileage and that these were not all reflected in the formula. The CAB concluded, however, that the public would best be served with a mileage-related fare formula that gave trips of equal distance essentially an equal fare. This would of course mean above-average profits on some routes (those that have a low unit cost, relative to stage length) and below-average profits for other routes (those that have high unit costs relative to length).

However, the CAB felt that the public as a whole would benefit from this averaging of profitability so long as the overall fare level did not produce excessive profits, and so long as elements of cost regarded as inefficient were disallowed. (Specifically, the CAB disallowed millions of dollars each year on the basis of load factors, utilization, and seat configuration levels that did not meet its standards.)

With deregulation, the concept of a mileage-related fare structure was replaced by the marketplace pragmatics of varying competitive pressures on different routes. Factors such as the following came into play to affect the fare levels in specific city pairs:

1. Carriers could newly enter into previously more profitable routes and settle for a fare level that would provide a more moderate profit, or even just a "contribution" over variable cost. (To a newly entering carrier, *any* contribution over marginal cost was more than the zero participation it previously had obtained on this route.)

2. New entrant carriers (with lower labor costs, the lower aircraft ownership cost of used planes, and possibly the lower cost of fewer amenities) could offer a fare lower than the norm previously prevailing on the route.

3. Carriers with cash deficit problems sometimes cut fares in the hope of stimulating a sudden surge of traffic and generating quick cash, even though this fell short of covering full costs.

4. Carriers able to participate indirectly in a given market (that is, via

one-stop or connecting service in a market served primarily on non-stops) could rationalize a very low fare for such one-stop or connection routing on the basis that this carrier would otherwise not get any of this traffic and that any small return would exceed the zero marginal cost of filling an empty seat.

5. A carrier might take an outright gamble on a very low fare, hoping that the level of the fare would deter other carriers from matching it. In this case the fare cutter could actually make out satisfactorily, getting a disproportionately high load factor because of having the best bargain on the route. For example, if the normal industry load factor on a given route was 55 percent, and if a fare-cutting carrier could get an 80 percent load factor by having an unmatched low fare, this load factor could, in itself, pay for a 31 percent fare differential even if all aspects of operating efficiency were identical for all carriers.

In some of these situations, the initiation of a fare reduction may have been related to the unusually favorable cost structure of the fare-cutting carriers, and in those cases the fully allocated cost of that carrier might be the basis for the fare action. In other cases, the fare-cutting carrier would be basing its action on some form of marginal cost pricing.

But, regardless of what level of cost recovery led to the initiation of a fare cut, the response to such action by the other carriers on the route has been nearly always a "marginal cost" decision. To the responding carrier, it is usually irrelevant whether the new, lower fare is adequate to cover its fully allocated cost. Even if the lower fare clearly falls below such full cost, the issue at this point is whether the responding carrier will lose more by refraining from matching (and merely flying empty seats) or by matching (and at least covering the marginal costs of handling the retained traffic).

By and large, airlines have concluded that it is less costly to match. Depending on the size and perceived market power of the fare-cutting carrier, the degree of the matching by the responding carriers might be total, or it might be partial (that is, only enough to keep the traffic loss contained). Sometimes the matching of lower fares has been accompanied by trip duration or other restrictive conditions. Very often, the matching has been on a "capacity-controlled" basis, where the responding carrier offers the lower fare on a selective basis for some portion of the seats on some flights while still seeking to preserve a full-fare level on much of its capacity as possible.

Sometimes, when the fare being matched was offered only at one airport within a metropolitan area (for example, as with People Express operating only at Newark), responding carriers would get into delicate balancing acts in their attempt to find the optimum basis for responding adequately without overreacting. This sometimes resulted in substantial differences in the fares quoted for different airports within the metropolitan area.

Given the nature of the competitive pressures, it was inevitable that fares would fall below fully allocated cost in the more competitive situations. In some fare-cutting situations even 100 percent load factors could not cover costs.

In view of the below-cost, competitively induced fares that have existed on some routes, carriers have had no choice but to attempt to offset this, as much as possible, with substantial fare increases on their less competitive routes. What has evolved is virtually a "two-tier" pricing pattern—lower fares on the more intensely competitive routes and higher fares on the less competitive ones. This explains the wide fare disparities with respect to the cross-section of markets in Exhibit 1-1. Wide fare disparity has sometimes encouraged circuitous routings, as passengers have sought ways to get the lowest fares.

In view of shifting competitive pressures, wide variation of pricing has existed not only between different routes, but also from month to month on the same route.

QUESTIONS

1. Complete Exhibit 1-1 using current year statistics. (See Methodology for Developing Fare Comparisons.) Break down the fare analysis sample by percentage of fare changes between 1978 and 1984 and between 1978 and the current year using the following table:

Fare Change Percent City	Number of Pairs	Percent of all City Pairs in Sample
− 20% to − 1 %		
0 to + 39 %		
+ 40% to + 79 %		
+ 80% to + 119 %		
+ 120% to + 139 %		
+ 140% to + 179 %		
+ 180% and over		
Total	70	100 %

2. Plot the fare per mile (cents) for the 70 city pairs on a graph similar to the following for April 1978, April 1984, and the current year. (Use three separate graphs.)

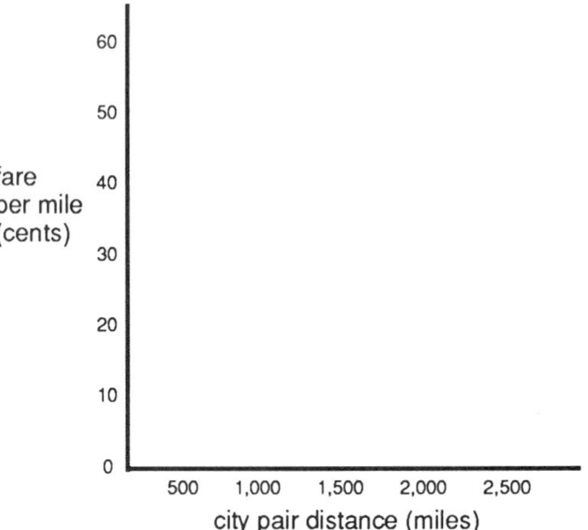

3. What observations can you make after reviewing Exhibit 1-1 and your graphical analysis? Are there any significant differences in the graphs for 1984 and the current year? What effect do you think the demise of such carriers as People Express, New York Air, and others have had on the current fare structure?

Background
Contract Refueling–Airline Division

2
JET SERVICE CENTER, INC.
General Aviation

In July 1988, management of Jet Service Center, Inc. was reviewing scheduling and contract refueling operations for the commercial air carriers they served at Metropolitan Airport. It had become apparent that the present refueling operations were inefficient. Although the problem was a long-standing one, management was particularly concerned at this time because costs had been increasing rapidly while revenues had leveled off. As a result, profits were being squeezed.

Employees were generally satisfied with their current work rules and management was concerned about the effect of changes on employee productivity. Jet Service Center had always been considered one of the top ten FBOs in the country according to surveys by the NBAA and *Professional Pilot* magazine. This high rating was largely attributable to the quality and dedication of the employees. However, management also felt that improved scheduling in the refueling operations could yield considerable cost savings.

BACKGROUND

Jet Service Center, Inc. (JSC) operates its facilities at Metropolitan Airport under a 30-year lease (to expire in 2005) with the Metropolis County Airport Authority. Under the terms of the lease, JSC provides airline and general aviation services. The airline division consisted of refueling air carrier flights under contracts with the airlines. The general aviation operations consists of services to private and corporate aircraft, including fueling services, collection of aircraft parking fees (as agent for the Airport Authority), maintenance and avionics repair and servicing, aircraft hangar and tie-down facilities, and other services such as airplane cleaning and baggage handling.

Competition

JSC has one other major competitor at Metropolitan Airport, Four Star Aero. The two firms are the only FBOs qualified and licensed by the county to fuel corporate and air carrier jet equipment at the airport. Several other smaller FBOs provide fueling for their own aircraft and some light single-engine transient aircraft. All other air carrier, corporate, and private aircraft are required to use JSC or Four Star Aero for refueling services. The only exception was in the case of air carriers who have the option of using one of the airport's licensed FBOs or of doing their own refueling. JSC refuels 5 of the 12 air carriers serving Metropolitan Airport; Four Star Aero refuels 4 including two small regional carriers; and 3 airlines refuel their own aircraft.

Facilities

JSC operates out of three locations at Metropolitan Airport: Hangar 26,

Hangar 28, and at the central terminal building. JSC's administrative offices and general aviation services lobby, dispatch counter, and pilot's lounge were located in Hangar 26. Aircraft storage and tie-down space, maintenance, and avionics repair and servicing are also provided in Hangar 26. In Hangar 28, JSC maintains its fleet of aircraft refueling vehicles plus its other ground servicing equipment. JSC maintains a small "line shack" in the main terminal building as a ready room for its airline division refueling staff.

Employees

JSC employs 52 people: 7 management personnel and 45 other employees divided into hangar and nonhangar groups. The nonhangar group includes:

1. Refuelers who can fuel either private, corporate, or carrier equipment, depending on their assignment.

2. Towmen who maneuver private and corporate aircraft.

3. Ramp attendants who greet general aviation customers, arrange for rental cars or limousines, and drive the two JSC station wagons to transport customers to and from their aircraft and to various locations in the area.

The hangar group includes:

1. Auto mechanics who perform maintenance work on all of JSC's vehicles (owned or leased).

2. Aircraft mechanics who service private and corporate aircraft.

3. Avionics technicians who service private and corporate aircraft.

4. Administrative personnel, including dispatchers, secretaries, and bookkeepers.

Labor-Management Relations

JSC's employees select a group of three representatives who meet with the general manager and two other management personnel once a year in what has become known as the "meet and confer" session. Through their representatives, employees have an opportunity to express their concerns regarding wages, benefits, and work rules. This process was established several years ago when there was a lot of talk by employees about establishing a union. At the time, one of the primary concerns of the refuelers was the number that should be used to refuel a plane. Previously, two refuelers had been used, but management felt that only one person was necessary. After much grumbling and several meetings with management, employees finally agreed to the change and subsequently received a 10% annual wage increase. In 1986 one of the major issues concerned employee classifications. The company wanted to eliminate all nonhangar group classifications (refueler, towman, and ramp attendant) so that any employee could perform all three tasks, but the employees wanted to maintain the classifications. Management finally withdrew this demand and signed the meet and confer agreement, which included another 10% annual wage increase. Since that time, relations with employees have generally been cordial. Employee morale has been good and their pay scale and benefits compare favorably with other comparably sized FBOs in this part of the country.

The seniority system is very important in scheduling shifts and overtime at JSC. When new shift schedules are made, they are given to the employees for the purpose of bidding. The most senior employees within each classification have the first option of the shift schedule they want. Overtime is also offered according to seniority. However, if overtime assignments are not accepted by senior employees, the most junior employees on the shift are required to accept the assignments. (See Exhibit 2–1 for the sections of the contract regarding hours of work and overtime.)

Revenue

The airline division generates about 40 percent of JSC's revenue at Metropolitan Airport; the general aviation operations provide the other 60 percent. Total revenue has been steady for the past several years at $3.75 million per year.

CONTRACT REFUELING—AIRLINE DIVISION

The air carriers serviced by JSC arrange contracts with JSC and an oil company. The oil company supplies the fuel at an agreed-on price (which the air carrier pays directly to the oil company) JSC acts as a "mediator," picking up fuel from the oil company's pumps and dispensing it into the planes. JSC's contract with an air carrier includes the total gallonage to be dispensed during the year and a fixed into-planing fee which JSC receives for each gallon pumped. The into-planing fee averages about 5 cents per gallon. JSC contracted to deliver a total of about 30,000,000 gallons during 1988.

The refueling arrangements are complicated by the fact that each oil

EXHIBIT 2-1 JSC Work Rules

A. Eight (8) consecutive hours in the twenty-four (24) hour period following the time an employee starts his or her scheduled shift, exclusive of an unpaid lunch period, will constitute a regular workday.

B. Forty (40) hours consisting of five (5) days of eight (8) hours each, worked within seven (7) consecutive days will constitute a regular workweek for an employee.

C. Overtime at the rate of time and one-half shall be paid for all hours worked in excess of eight (8) in a workday.

D. Overtime at the rate of time and one-half shall be paid for all hours worked in excess of forty (40) in an employee's scheduled workweek, and for all hours worked on his or her regularly scheduled first day off and overtime at the rate of double time for all hours worked on his or her regularly scheduled second day off, if the employee also worked on the scheduled first day off.

. . .

F. Lunch periods shall be completed between three and one-half (3 1/2) and five and one-half (5 1/2) hours on each shift. If the Employer requires an employee to work through such lunch period, he or she will be paid at the rate of time and one-half for time worked during such lunch period and, in addition, will be given fifteen (15) minutes for lunch at least two (2) hours before his or her quitting time.

. . .

H. An employee called back to perform work after completion of his or her scheduled hours on a workday and after he or she has left the Employer's premises shall be paid at the applicable overtime rate for not less than four (4) hours.

An employee who reports for work as scheduled without having been notified in advance by the Employer not to report shall receive not less than eight (8) hours of pay at his or her regular straight-time rate, unless the employee on his or her own initiative fails to complete the scheduled hours, is sent home for just cause, is excused from such hours at his or her own request, or no work is available as a result of a work stoppage or interference with operations in connection with a labor dispute.

. . .

Q. An employee who works overtime will be allowed eight (8) hours off duty between the time of completion of his or her overtime assignment and the start of his or her next scheduled shift, and will not suffer a loss of regular pay for reporting late for such next shift as a result of this allowance.

company requires JSC to dispense fuel utilizing trucks with the oil company's markings. This requirement was not a problem in the past since all the airlines JSC serviced had contracts with Shale Oil. However, recently Great Lakes Airlines contracted with Evvron Oil to supply their fuel. JSC estimated that, starting in January, at least one Evvron truck would be needed to perform Great Lakes' refueling operations.

Equipment

JSC uses seven fuel trucks in the airline refueling operations. Five have capacities of 8,400 gallons and two have capacities of 5,100 gallons. The larger trucks are leased from the oil companies at a cost of $2,400 per truck per month. JSC owns one of its smaller trucks and leases the remaining 5,100 gallon truck at a cost of $1,500 per month. Operating and maintenance costs amount to about $10,000 per truck per year for the larger trucks and about $6,000 per truck per year for the smaller trucks. This includes fuel and oil for operating the trucks and parts and labor for maintaining them. It does not include the costs of the refuelers.

Fuel Requirements

Although the total number of gallons to be pumped during the year is contracted, the specific amount of fuel to be pumped into a plane each day is decided daily by the airlines. The amount of fuel required depends on the type of plane, its destination, its passenger load, and weather conditions. Since passenger loads and weather have only a limited effect on fuel requirements, the amount of fuel a particular flight takes from day to day varies within narrow limits, because the plane type and destination is almost always the same for a particular flight.

The airlines usually wait until a few hours before departure time before determining the exact amount of fuel they want for each flight. By so doing, they take advantage of the most current information about the weather and passenger loads. Occasionally, fuel requests are changed while passengers are boarding the plane. Once airline personnel have determined the amount of fuel they want for a particular flight, the amount is written on a fuel request form that is held by the airline dispatchers until someone from JSC picks it up. A refueler cannot fuel a plane without the proper request form, which is prepared in triplicate. One copy is left with the dispatcher, one copy is for JSC's use, and one copy is left either with personnel at the airline's gate or with the pilot after refueling is completed. (See Exhibit 2–2 for the various types of air craft and the amounts of fuel pumped by JSC.)

Flight Schedules

In the contract refueling operation, JSC services 49 commercial flights per day, Monday through Friday. Fewer flights are scheduled and

EXHIBIT 2–2 Contract Airline Refueling

Airline	Type of Aircraft	Uplift Gallonage Range
Coastal Air	DC-9	1000–1500
Trans Continent	DC-9	1500–2400
	B-727	2500–4500
	DC-10	2000–3000
Mid America	B-727	2500–3500
	B-737	1000–1400
National Air	B-737	1000–1300
Great Lakes	B-727	1600–2000

serviced on the weekend, 36 on Saturday and 42 on Sunday. Two large boards (coinciding with JSC's two daily shifts) are maintained in the line shack with a complete schedule of the estimated time of arrival (ETA) and estimated time of departure (ETD) for all the flights that JSC services. Major airline schedule changes occur on a quarterly basis. The Monday-Friday schedule of airline arrivals and departures for the fall of 1988, including aircraft type, is provided in Exhibit 2–3.

Two planes serviced by JSC are on the ground overnight. However, these planes cannot be refueled until morning since the airlines want as much time as possible to determine passenger loads and weather conditions. The refueling request forms for these planes are usually available at 0600 and the refuelers generally begin refueling these planes about 0630.

Performance Criteria

The essential performance criteria for the refueling operation are on-time service, safety, and quality fuel.

1. *On-time service.* JSC's policy is to meet a plane as soon as it arrives at its gate and complete the refueling operation as quickly as possible. They could continue pumping fuel into a plane until just before it is ready to pull away from the gate without causing any delay. But JSC's management prefers that the refuelers complete the refueling at least five minutes before departure time.

EXHIBIT 2-3 Airline Schedule—Monday through Friday

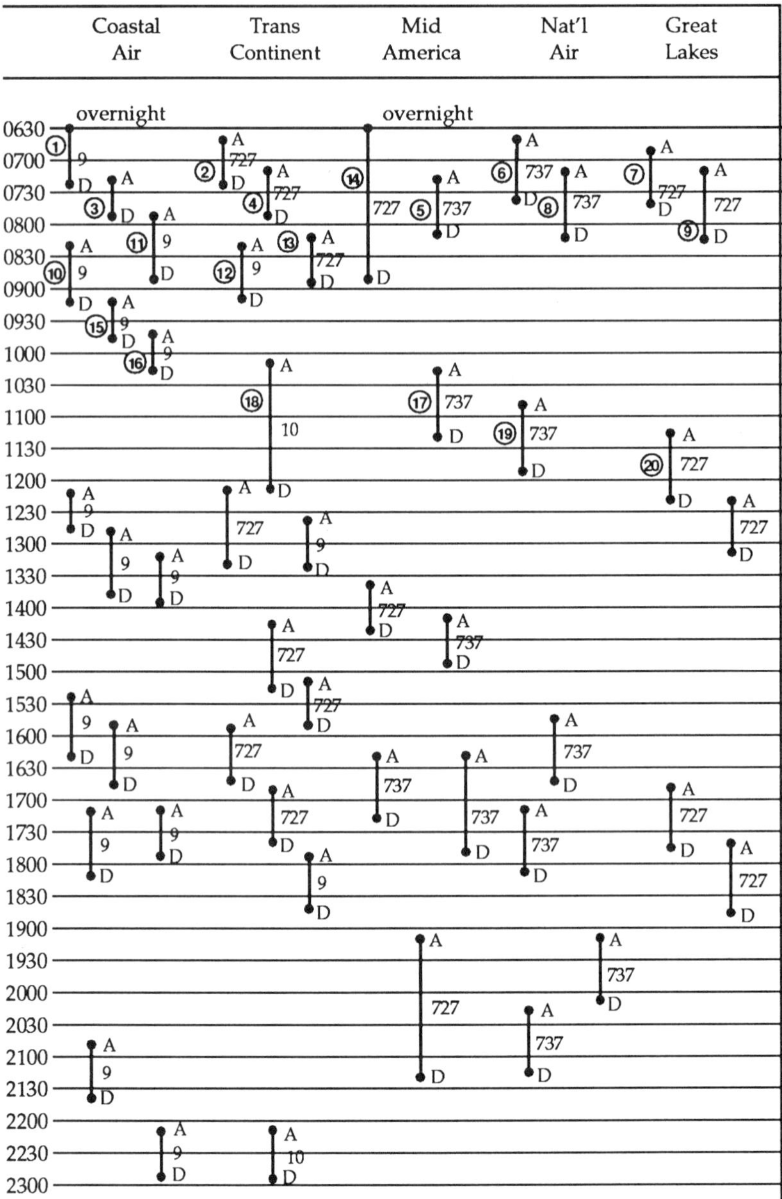

Time	Arrivals	Departures
0630	5	0
0700	5	2
0730	1	4
0800	3	3
0830	0	3
0900	1	2
0930	1	1
1000	2	1
1030	1	0
1100	1	1
1130	0	1
1200	3	2
1230	2	1
1300	1	3
1330	1	2
1400	2	1
1430	0	1
1500	2	1
1530	3	1
1600	2	1
1630	2	3
1700	3	1
1730	2	4
1800	0	2
1830	0	2
1900	2	0
1930	0	0
2000	1	1
2030	1	0
2100	0	2
2130	0	1
2200	2	0
2230	0	2
2300		

	Coastal Air	Trans Continent	Mid America	Nat'l Air	Great Lakes	Arrivals	Departures
Arrivals	15	13	8	7	6	49	
Departures	15	13	8	7	6		49

Code: A—arrival; D—departure; 9—DC-9; 10—DC-10; 727—B-727; 737—B-737.

2. *Safety.* Refuelers maneuver the trucks carefully to avoid collisions with the planes. When refuelers back their trucks into or out of fueling positions, they are required to have someone assist them. However, if a refueler can maneuver in and pull away from a plane by driving straight forward, he or she is allowed to do so without assistance.

3. *Quality fuel.* The refuelers have to make sure that the proper fuel is dispensed into the plane and that the fuel contains no contaminants. This means that fuel trucks must be emptied every morning to remove any water that may have condensed inside the tanks overnight.

In addition to the major criteria outlined above, JSC's management also wants the refuelers to provide their services in a courteous manner.

Organization of Refueling Operations

The contract refueling operations are performed utilizing a pooling concept. Both manpower and trucks are assigned to a pool. The "pool" for refuelers is the small 8' x 18' line shack located in the airport terminal. Parking for the fuel trucks is provided near the taxiways about 700 yards from the pool. JSC was unable to secure permission from the Airport Authority to move the truck parking closer to the terminal. However, a driver could stop the truck momentarily at the pool to see if it would be needed again immediately. In addition, one or two spots were used near the pool (about 50 yards away) for trucks that would be needed within two or three minutes.

In the refueling operations, one lead refueler, one "floater," and several regular refuelers are used. The lead refueler is responsible for giving the refuelers assignments throughout the day. The work must be coordinated so that the planes are serviced without delay and so that the fuel trucks are filled again (topped) when they become too low on fuel for further refueling. The lead refueler can also refuel planes. He does not top trucks, however, because this assignment would take him away from the pool for too long.

The "floater" is a refueler who drives a station wagon. He or she picks up the fueling request forms from the dispatchers, drives refuelers to and from fuel trucks, and helps refuelers back the fuel trucks into and out of position near the planes.

The regular refuelers report to the pool and wait for assignments from the lead. A refueler might be assigned to refuel a plane or top a truck that was too low on fuel to be used in another refueling. Often the lead gives a refueler two or three assignments at one time. In 1988, a lead refueler earned approximately $14.00 an hour; a refueler earned an average $11.50 an hour. In addition to regular pay, fringe benefits amounted to about 25 percent of straight-time pay.

Communications with the Airlines

The refuelers have no contact with the tower and no formal communication system with the individual airlines to learn in advance whether the planes will arrive on schedule. JSC previously had communication systems in the pool for all the airlines, but these were eliminated when the airlines switched to closed-circuit televisions to show arrival and departure times. JSC did not tap into the television communication system because facilities would have had to be provided for five separate channels. Management estimated that these channels would cost about $6,500 to $7,000 each to install. Furthermore, the system often was not updated soon enough to be useful and did not provide information about when planes were cleared to land and when they had actually landed.

Normally, however, JSC knows that a plane is on the ground before a refueler is dispatched to the plane's gate. Airline personnel often (but not always) contact the lead refueler in the ready room by phone if planes are behind schedule. In addition, the dispatchers usually know when planes will arrive late and they inform the person from JSC who picks up the fuel request forms. This information reduces the number of times refuelers make trips to a gate to discover that the flight has not yet arrived.

Communication among the Refuelers

The lead refueler and the floater use walkie-talkies in communicating with each other. The floater frequently uses the walkie-talkie to inform the lead of the flights for which there are fueling request forms, the amount of fuel the planes will need and whether the planes will arrive on schedule. This allows the lead to make assignments to the refuelers without always having to wait for the floater to bring the fuel request forms. By driving around, the floater keeps track of the refueling of each plane and knows when it is time to help a refueler back a truck near an aircraft and when a refueler needs to be driven to the ready room from the fuel truck parking area. The floater also uses the walkie-talkie to inform the lead when refuelers have finished their assignments. The lead, in turn, uses the walkie-talkie to ask the floater to pick up refuelers and drive them out to the fuel trucks or to request the floater to give a refueler another assignment.

JSC's management considered installing radios in the fuel trucks to improve the efficiency of the refueling operation but decided against it, "simply because the radios would be stolen."

The lead refueler uses the airline schedule, information from the floater, and information obtained by phone to determine when to dispatch refuelers. The lead uses the fueling request forms plus information obtained directly from the refuelers and the floater to keep track of the amount of fuel in each truck to determine when a truck needs to be topped.[1]

Refueling Process

When a refueler is assigned to refuel a plane, he or she first checks to see if a truck is already available at or near the pool. Frequently, however, all trucks are in the regular parking area. In that case, the lead assigns the floater to drive the refueler out to the trucks. The refueler picks up the necessary fuel request form either from the lead or the floater.

After the refueler is driven to the parked trucks, he or she drives a truck to the gate where the assigned plane is scheduled to arrive. Occasionally, however, the plane is not at the gate when the refueler arrives with the truck. In that case the refueler checks with personnel at the gate to ascertain the plane's expected arrival time. If the plane is to arrive in less than five minutes, the refueler waits and then refuels the plane. If the wait is to be longer than five minutes, however, the refueler drives the truck back to the pool to see whether it is needed elsewhere. If the truck is not needed immediately but will be needed within two or three minutes, it is parked in a spot near the pool (if space is available). Otherwise, it is taken back to the regular parking area, usually after the driver requests that the floater come out to pick him or her up.

Sometimes a refueler uses a fuel truck that does not have enough fuel to supply the assigned plane and the lead is unaware of it. Ideally, under those circumstances, the refueler would start pumping fuel into the plane and then phone the lead from the gate to request a backup truck. Occasionally, however, the refueler does not check in advance to see if there is enough fuel to refuel the plane, so he or she has to call the lead after the fuel truck is empty. When this happens, it sometimes causes a departure delay.

Often, however, the lead assigns a truck that he or she already knows is too low on fuel to refuel the assigned plane. In this case a backup truck is also assigned. This type of assignment reduces the number of times the fuel trucks need to be topped with fuel.

Topping Trucks

Once a refueling operation is completed, the driver checks to see if enough fuel remains in the truck to do further refueling.[2] The lead keeps track of the amount of fuel in each truck and knows whether the fuel truck needs to be refilled after the refueler finishes the assignment. In

---

[1]The lead is not always able to keep track of the fuel in each truck, especially during peak times or when the lead has given a refueler a series of assignments.

[2]The fuel farm, located on the far side of the airport, consists of several large fuel pumps that supply various kinds of aviation fuel. The fuel farm is maintained by the oil companies.

this case, he or she usually assigns the driver to drive the fuel truck immediately to the fuel farm to be topped. If the truck needs to be refilled and the lead is not aware of it, the refueler drives the truck back to the pool and informs the lead, who assigns either this driver or another one to take the truck to the fuel farm to be topped. But if the truck still has enough fuel to refuel another plane, the refueler either goes to another refueling assignment or drives the truck back to the pool or directly to the regular parking area, depending on the assignment.

Time Requirements

About two to three minutes are required to ride out to the trucks in the regular parking area. Another two to three minutes are required to drive to the plane's gate for the refueling operation. Refueling can usually be completed in about 20 minutes. Following the refueling, another two to three minutes are required to drive the truck back to the parking area. If the refueler has to walk in from the regular parking area (this rarely occurs), it takes about 10 minutes. Topping off a truck takes about 40 minutes. About half the time is spent simply driving the two and one-half miles to and from the fuel farm.

Staffing and Shift Schedules

The contract refueling operations use a staff of 14 refuelers. Each refueler serves five shifts per week. The shifts are eight and one-half hours each (eight paid hours) with a half-hour for a meal, two 10-minute breaks, and a 10-minute cleanup period at the end of the shift. However, since employees have a considerable amount of idle time during their shifts, breaks are not formally scheduled. Meals are taken between the third and fifth hours of the employee's shift. The aggregate shift schedule is shown in Exhibit 2–4; the schedule for the individual shifts (which the refuelers bid for by seniority) is shown in Exhibit 2–5. The refuelers range in age from about 20 to 60 and in length of employment from 2 to 25 years. The average length of employment is about eight and one-half years.

Overtime

JSC does not schedule any shifts to exceed eight and one-half hours, but they budget for overtime wages at about 10 percent of the straight-time wages paid during the year. Overtime is caused by three main factors:

1. Airline schedules are thrown off occasionally by bad weather and congestion at major hub airports. When this happens, the flights began arriving late and the entire schedule is usually delayed by several hours. This often means that refuelers have to remain at the airport to handle the later flights. Bad weather disrupts the flight schedules approximately 36 days a year.

EXHIBIT 2-4 Staffing Schedule—Airline Division

Shift	Number of Refuelers per Shift							
	Mon	*Tues*	*Wed*	*Thurs*	*Fri*	*Sat*	*Sun*	*Total*
Day	6	6	6	6	6	4	5	39
Evening	5	5	5	5	5	3	3	31
Total	11	11	11	11	11	7	8	70*

*14 refuelers (incl. 2 leads) x 5 shifts each = 70

EXHIBIT 2-5 Individual Shift Schedule—Airline Division

Shift	Number of Refuelers per Shift						
	Mon	*Tues*	*Wed*	*Thurs*	*Fri*	*Sat*	*Sun*
Day (0630–1450)							
1. Lead Refueler	D	D	D	D			D
2. Refueler	D	D			D	D	D
3. Refueler		D	D	D	D	D	
4. Refueler			D	D	D	D	D
5. Refueler	D	D	D			D	D
6. Refueler	D	D	D	D	D		
7. Refueler	D	D	D	D	D		
8. Refueler	D	E		D	D		D
Evening (1430–2350)							
9. Lead Refueler	E	E	E	E			E
10. Refueler	E	E			E	E	E
11. Refueler		E	E	E	E	E	
12. Refueler	E	E	E	E	E		
13. Refueler	E		E	E	E	E	
14. Refueler	E		E	E	E		E
Total	11	11	11	11	11	7	8

2. Overtime is paid on holidays at 2.5 times the straight-time rate. There are 11 paid holidays each year.

3. Overtime is also incurred to cover unscheduled absences by refuelers. The absenteeism rate (currently about 8 percent) has increased substantially in recent years and is seen as one of the main contributers to excessive overtime wages which currently amount to about 15 percent of straight-time wages.

Alternatives under Consideration

In rescheduling the refueling operations, management is considering several alternatives. Refuelers could be assigned to specific trucks, to specific airlines, to top fuel trucks only, or a combination of these alternatives. Management's goals are to achieve maximum utilization of manpower and to improve cost control. They hope to be able to reduce maintenance costs and the number of trucks and people required. If changes mean that fewer people would be required, employees would not be laid off, but the work force could be reduced through attrition.

Management feels that by assigning employees to specific trucks, the employees would develop pride in their vehicles and would take better care of them. Management would also have greater control since they would know who was responsible for a given truck in case any damage or other problem occurred. Management feels that this plan would reduce truck maintenance costs by 5 to 10 percent. By assigning specific people to airlines, management hopes to provide better service to the airlines and hopes that refuelers would get to know the flight schedule for the planes they are assigned to refuel.

Management realizes, of course, that there are risks in assigning people to trucks and to airlines because JSC would lose some of the flexibility the pool provided; also workers might refuse even in emergencies to do refueling for planes other than their own assigned airlines. So they wonder whether they should simply try to utilize the pool concept better. They know that on several occasions the refuelers have been able to accomplish the refueling of all planes with ease when an unscheduled absence occurs and a replacement is not called in.

Implementation

Management is not only concerned about how to reschedule the refueling operations, but also about how to implement whatever decision is made. They feel that implementation would be the biggest problem. They first must decide whether the changes should be made on a piecemeal basis because they could experiment a little and try to determine the best system. Furthermore, they could present the problem and some of their ideas to employees and perhaps get their support. They feel that if the employees had the opportunity to influence the final decision they might not resist the changes so much. Moreover, they might make some good suggestions about improving operations. However, if employees believe that management is only trying to lay people off whenever any changes are made, their cooperation might be difficult to get.

At any rate, the decision must be made soon because new schedules come up for bidding in August and the decision has to be worked out before then. Management feels that any changes should be made in the summer. Employes could slow down operations if they don't like a change, causing delays to the airlines. Management believes that if changes were made in the winter and employees don't like them, they could probably shut JSC down. Delays are much more serious and difficult to handle in the winter than in the summer. After enough delays, the airlines might cancel their contracts.

With all the foregoing facts and considerations in mind, management tries to work out both the changes that should be made in the contract refueling operations and the methods that should be used in implementing those changes.

QUESTIONS

1a. Complete the following income statement for the Airline Division.

Revenue: ________ x ________ = ________

	Est. annual gallons		Into-planing fee		Est. annual airline div. revenue
Revenue:	________	x	________	=	________

Expenses:

Labor		Lead refuelers	and	Refuelers		
Number	x	________		________		
Wage/hr	x	________		________		
hr/wk	x	________		________		
wk/yr	x	________		________		
Fringe benefits	x	________		________		
Total	=	________		________	=	________ Total wages and fringe benefits

Overtime ________ % x ________ Straight-time wages (excl. fringe benefits) = ________

Total labor = ________

Equipment (lease cost)

		Large trucks	and	Small trucks		
Number	x	________		________		
Cost/mo	x	________		________		
12 mo	=	________		________	=	________ Total equipment cost

Operations and maintenance cost

		Large trucks	and	Small trucks		
Number	x	________		________		
Cost/yr	x	________		________		
Total	=	________		________	=	________ Tot. oper. and mtc. cost

Total expenses	=	________
Gross profit	=	________
Overhead and nonoper. expenses	=	$485,000
Net profit	=	________

b.Give a brief analysis of the statement.

2. Determine the time requirements for work to be performed.

   a. Estimated gallons per flight

      (1) Flights per week (M–F) ________

      Saturday ________

      Sunday ________

      Total ________

      (2) Est. flights per year ________

      (3) Est. tot. gallons/yr ________

      (4) Est. gallons/flight ________

   b. Estimated # of flights before retopping a large truck

      (1) Capacity of a large truck ________ gallons

      (2) ÷ est. gallons/flight (a4) ________

      (3) Average # of flights ________ (round to nearest whole #)

c. Estimated # of flights before retopping a small truck

(1) Capacity of a small truck __________ gallons

(2) ÷ est. gallons/flight (a4) __________

(3) Average # of flights __________ (round to nearest whole #)

d. Average number of flights before a truck will need to refill

(1) Number of large trucks __________

(2) x average # of flights (b3) __________

(3) Total = __________

(4) Number of small trucks __________

(5) x average # of flights (c3) __________

(6) Total = __________

(7) (d3) + (d6) = __________

(8) (d7) ÷ total number of trucks__________ = __________ (round up to next nearest whole # because we have underestimated and most trucks are large)

e. Number of refills per day

(1) Weekday flights per day

________ = __________

(2) Saturday flights________ ÷ (d8)_______ = __________

(3) Sunday flights ________ = __________ (round to nearest whole number)

f. Time to refuel trucks per week (retopping)

(1) Weekday refills (e1)

_______ x _______ = _______ x _______ = _______ min

(2) Saturday refills (e2) _______ av. min. = _______ min

(3) Sunday refills(e3) _______ to retop = _______ min

Total minutes/week _______

g. Time to refuel planes per week (refueling)

(1) Weekday flts. per day

_______ x _______ = _______ x _______ = _______ min

(2) Saturday flights _______ av. min = _______ min

(3) Sunday flights _______ to refuel = _______ min

Total minutes/week _______

h. Time to get and return trucks (positioning)

(1) Weekday flts. per day

_______ x _______ = _______ x _______ = _______ min

(2) Saturday flights _______ av. min = _______ min

(3) Sunday flights _______ to position* = _______ min

Total minutes/week _______

*Ride to truck 2–3 minutes; drive to plane 2–3 minutes; drive back 2–3 minutes; drive to line shack 2-3 minutes (10 minutes if walking). Use an average of 12 minutes.

i. Total time worked (by function)

(1) Retopping trucks _______ min _______ %

(2) Refueling planes _______ min _______ %

(3) Positioning trucks _______ min _______ %

Total minutes/week _______ 100 %

j. Total time worked (by day)

	Typical wkday	Saturday	Sunday
(1) Retopping	________ min	________ min	________ min
(2) Refueling	________ min	________ min	________ min
(3) Positioning	________ min	________ min	________ min
Total	________ min	________ min	________ min

(4) Saturday as a % of typical weekday________ %

(5) Sunday as a % of typical weekday________ %

3a. Estimate the utilization of available manpower.

Assuming that 2 people in the work force are used as lead refuelers (one per shift) and 2 are used as floaters (one per shift); 10 are available to perform the refueling task. In a given day there are 8.5 hours per man less 1/2 hour for lunch, two 10-minute breaks, and a 10-minute cleanup. This leaves 7.5 work hours per person per day.

(1) Regular time available

__________ x 7.5 x 5 day/wk x 60 min/hr = __________

\# of refuelers — Tot. min/wk

(2) Overtime available

This is difficult to calculate since we are only given overtime payments (at 15% of straight-time wages). Some is at 1.5x, and some, on holidays, etc., is at 2.5x. Assume that this averages out at 2x, so overtime hours are, therefore, 15/2 = 7.5% of regular hours.

__________ x 7.5 = __________

Tot. minutes — Tot. minutes/wk

(3) Total time available

__________ + __________ = __________

Regular time — Overtime — Tot. minutes/wk

(4) Utilization of manpower

________	÷	________	=	________%
Tot. work req. min (2i)		Tot. time avail. min (3a)		Manpower utilization

b. Does the utilization appear to be low? Is 100 percent utilization possible? 80 percent? 70 percent? What is the cost saving by increasing utilization? Why do you think it is difficult to increase average utilization in aviation firms such as JSC?

4. Estimate the utilization of trucks

________	x	________	x 7 days x 60 min =	________
# of trucks		hrs avail. (0630–2300)		Tot. minutes/wk

________	÷	________	=	________%
Tot. work req. mins. (2i)		Tot. time avail. minutes		Truck utilization

5a. Is there any possibility of eliminating trucks based on the schedules in Exhibits A and B on the following page which cover the period 0630-1200 (the first major peak in flights—20 out of 49)?

b. Develop an alternate schedule. Can you eliminate any trucks based on your schedule? (Remember that starting in January, one Evvron truck must be used to refuel Great Lakes flights.)

6. Why do the air carriers use FBOs such as JSC for refueling? Why don't the air carriers or oil companies do it themselves?

7a. What do you think about management's idea to eliminate the pooling concept and assign refuelers to specific trucks, specific airlines, to retop fuel trucks, or a combination of these alternatives? (See Alternative under Consideration.)

b. Management considered installing radios in the fuel trucks to improve the efficiency of the refueling operation but decided against it. (See Communication among the Refuelers.) Was this a good decision? Why?

8. What operating rules is JSC using? Do they make sense? What rules did you use in developing your alternate schedule in Question 5b? (See Refueling Process and Topping trucks.)

9. What can JSC do to improve efficiency and control over their refueling operations?

EXHIBIT A Possible Gallons Pumped by Plane 0630–1200

Taking a required time for refueling to be 30 minutes before departure, the gallonage requirements for planes departing may be established from Exhibit 2–3.

Approx. departure time by:	Plane #				
	1	2	3	4	5
0730	(1) DC-9 1250 gals.	(2) B-727 3500			
0800	(3) DC-9 1250	(4) B-727 3500	(5) B-737 1200	(6) B-737 1150	(7) B-727 1800
0830	(8) B-737 1150	(9) B-727 1800			
0900	(10) DC-9 1250	(11) DC-9 1250	(12) DC-9 1950	(13) B-727 3500	(14) B-727 3000
0930					
1000	(15) DC-9 1250				
1030	(16) DC-9 1250				
1100					
1130	(17) B-737 1200				
1200	(18) DC-10 2500	(19) B-737 1150	(20) B-727 1800		

EXHIBIT B Possible Truck Schedule 0630–1200

The figures shown in Exhibit B are total gallons withdrawn from truck.

Gallons withdrawn by:	Trucks (8400 gallons)					(5100 gallons)	
	1	2	3	4	5	6	7
0730	(1) 1250	(2) 3500					
0800			(3) 1250	(4) 3500	(5) 1200	(6) 1150	(7) 1800
0830	(8) (+1150)2400	(9) (+1800)5300					
0900			(10) (+1250)2500	(11) (+1250)4750	(12) (+1950)3150	(13) (+3500)4650	(14) (+3000)4800
0930						Sent to retop	Sent to retop
1000	(15) (+1250)3650						
1030		(16) (+1250)6550					
1100							
1130		(17) (+1200)7750					
1200	(20) (+1800)5450	Sent to retop		(18) (+2500)7250	(19) (+1150)4300		
1230				Sent to retop			

Background
Rotavonni's Organizational Philosophy
The Eagle Airways Concept: The Philosophy Organizationalized

3
EAGLE AIRWAYS
Airline Organization

BACKGROUND

Eagle Airways (EA) is a large regional carrier operating out of Midwest City, located approximately 75 miles from one of the busiest hub airports in the country. Under the leadership of Joe Rotavonni, its founder and president, Eagle Airways has carved out a distinct niche for itself by catering to the business traveler. The airline flies DC 9-10s reconfigured from the usual 85 2 x 3 seating to 60 2 x 2 seating with extra wide seats and additional compartments for carry-on luggage. Gourmet meals are served on china with complimentary wine. Hundreds of complimentary letters to the carrier attest to passenger appreciation of extra legroom, carry-on luggage facilities, excellent on-time performance, no lost or damaged baggage, exemplary in-flight service, and particularly the carrier's outstanding people.

It was Rotavonni's idea to develop something unique:

> Our schedules are designed around business travelers out of Midwest City to major destinations. We give the business traveler a place to work at competitive coach fares. We do this by hubbing from secondary markets with smaller aircraft. For example, we fly about 70,000 passengers a year between Midwest City and Boston. It is a small market by major airline standards but it is big enough for us to serve effectively with our 60-passenger aircraft.

Eagle Airways recently completed a five-year growth plan that increased its fleet to 17 aircraft—eight DC 9-10s and nine DC 9-30s. Charter flights, primarily flown on late evenings and weekends, have grown significantly in recent years and the company now has contracts to fly several college athletic teams. On winter weekends, flights are scheduled to Sarasota, Orlando, Daytona Beach, and Fort Lauderdale.

In 1988 the airline completed a $3.5 million refurbishment of its seven gates and other facilities at Midwest City International Airport. Approximately 600 employees including its administrative staff are located at the Midwest City base. Another 800 employees are located around Eagle's system.

ROTAVONNI'S ORGANIZATIONAL PHILOSOPHY

Rotavonni worked for two major carriers in his 20-year airline career, which included a wide range of positions in finance and marketing as he worked up the corporate ladder. Coming from a background of very large, highly structured organizations that allowed little room for personal innovation, Rotavonni felt that there was a better way to run an airline. At least as important was his strong conviction that people were basically good and trustworthy, that they could be more effectively organized, and if properly trained, were likely to be creative and productive:

> I guess the single predominant reason that I cared about starting a new company was to try and develop a better way for people to work together . . . that's where the name Eagle Airways came from. It denotes strength, pride, fidelity and a long-term commitment. . . . It drives everything else that we do. . . . Most large carriers, with their highly unionized work force believe that people must be managed and controlled to make sure that they work. At Eagle Airways, employees are trusted to do a good job until they prove they definitely won't.

While Rotavonni recognized that his stance was contrary to the majority of organized structures in the United States, he rejected any insinuation that he was optimistic or soft: "I'm not a goody two-shoes person, I don't view myself as a social scientist, as a minister, as a do-gooder. I perceive myself as a hard-nosed businessman, whose ambitions and aspirations have to do with providing goods and services to other people for a return."

In addition, however, he wanted EA to serve as a role model for other organizations, a concept that carried with it the desire to have an external impact and to contribute to the world's debate about "how the hell to do things well, with good purpose, good intent, and good results for everybody. To me, that's good business, a good way to live. It makes sense, it's logical, it's hopeful, so why not do it?"

Prior to starting service, Rotavonni and the other managing officers spent a lot of time discussing their ideas about the "right" way to run an airline. Early on, they retained an outside management consultant to help them work together effectively as a management team and to articulate the principles to which they could commit themselves and their company. Over time, the principles evolved into a list of six "precepts," which were referred to continually in devising and explaining company policies, hiring and training new recruits, structuring and assigning tasks. These precepts were: (1) service and commitment to growth of employees; (2) best provider of air transportation; (3) highest quality of management; (4) role model for other airlines and other businesses; (5) simplicity; (6) maximization of profits.

From Rotavonni's philosophy as well as these precepts and a myriad of how-to-do-it ideas, a set of strategies began to evolve. According to Eagle's management consultant, the "path" theory was the modus operandi—management would see what route people took to get somewhere, then pave the paths that had been worn naturally to make them more visible.

Thus, early in its corporate life, the company could articulate fairly clearly a set of strategies that had become "the concept," the way things were done at Eagle Airways.

THE EAGLE AIRWAYS CONCEPT: THE PHILOSOPHY OPERATIONALIZED

The Eagle Airways business concept was broken down and operationalized into three sets of strategies: marketing, cost, and people.

Marketing Strategy

Fundamental to Eagle's initial marketing strategy was its view of air travel as a commodity product for which consumers had little or no brand loyalty. Eagle Airways defines its own version of that product as a quality, competitively priced air trip. The marketing strategy was to build and maintain passenger volume by offering competitive fares and frequent, dependable service on previously overpriced, underserved routes. In keeping with this strategy, the following tactics were adopted:

Competitive Fares. On any given route, Eagle's fares were at or below the standard fares prevailing prior to EA's announcement of service on that route. On average, peak fares ran from 15 to 20 percent below the competition's standard fares and 25 to 30 percent below during off-peak hours (after 6 P.M. and on weekends).

Convenient Flight Schedules. Eagle Airways focused on one-stop service from secondary hubs, typically underserved by the major carriers; for example, Milwaukee to Philadelphia and Indianapolis to New York. For any route that its planes flew, EA tried to offer the most frequent flight schedule. With competitive fares and frequent flights, EA could broaden its market segment beyond those of established airlines to include passengers who ordinarily would have used other forms of transportation. In an effort to expand the size of the air travel market, EA's ads announcing service in new cities were pitched to automobile drivers, bus riders, business fliers who previously had to connect to major hubs such as Chicago O'Hare, and even those who tended not to travel at all. Eagle hoped to capture most of the increase as well as some share of the pre-existing market for each route.

Regionwide Identity. Eagle set out to establish a formidable image. Serving secondary markets in the Midwest, its route structure focused on cities along the eastern seaboard as well as Memphis, Little Rock, Atlanta, and Pittsburgh. Large established airlines could easily wage price wars and successfully compete with a new airline in any one city, but they would probably have to absorb some losses and would be hard pressed to mount such a campaign on several fronts at once, particularly from the secondary markets served by Eagle.

Pitch to "Smart" Air Travelers. In keeping with its product definition, EA's ads did not seek to identify Eagle as exotic, entertaining, or fun to fly. Instead, it was depicted as the smart travel choice for smart, cost-conscious, service-minded busy travelers who depended on on-time performance. The ads were filled with consumer information, as well as information about EA's smart, caring employees and policies. Unlike most carriers, every Eagle Airways plane had roomy overhead compartments for passengers' baggage thereby saving them money, time, and the potential inconvenience of loss.

Positive Atmosphere. Rotavonni's long-term marketing strategy was to make flying Eagle Airways the most pleasant and memorable travel experience possible. The goal was for passengers to arrive at their destination feeling very well served. Thus, Eagle Airways' ultimate marketing strategy was to staff every position with competitive, sensitive, respectful, upbeat, high-energy people who would create a contagious positive atmosphere. The message to staff and customers alike was: "At Eagle Airways, attitude is as important as altitude."

Cost Structure

Eagle's cost structure was not based on a clear-cut formula so much as on an attitude that encouraged the constant, critical examination of every aspect of the business. According to Rotavonni, the management team looked for every possible way to do things more simply and efficiently. Cost savings measures affecting every aspect of the business included the following:

Aircraft. Since fuel is a major cost item for any carrier, Eagle chose, redesigned, and deployed its aircraft with fuel efficiency in mind. Its twin-engine Douglas DC-9 aircraft were thought to be the most fuel-efficient planes for their mission in the industry. The first-class section was eliminated and overhead racks were expanded to accommodate more carry-on baggage. The planes were decorated to convey a modern image of quality and roominess.

Eagle scheduled their aircraft to squeeze the most possible flying time out of them, approximately 10.5 hours per plane per day, compared with an industry average of close to 7 hours. Finally, aircraft major maintenance work was performed by other carriers on a contract basis, a practice seen as less expensive than hiring a base maintenance staff.

Low Labor Costs. Labor is typically a carrier's major operating expense. Though salaries were generally competitive and in some cases above industry norms, Eagle's labor costs were relatively small. The belief was that if every employee were intelligent, well-trained, flexible, and motivated to work hard, fewer people (as much as one-third fewer) would be needed than most airlines employed.

Eagle kept its work force deliberately lean and expected it to work hard. Each employee, carefully selected after an extensive screening process, received training in multiple functions (ticketing, reservations, ground operations, and so on) and was extensively cross-utilized, depending on the company's needs at any given time. If a bag had to be carried to a plane, whoever was heading toward the plane would carry the bag. Thus, peaks and valleys could be handled efficiently. This was in sharp contrast with other airlines, which hired people into one of a variety of distinct "classes in craft" (such as flight attendants, reservations, baggage), each of which had a fairly rigid job description, was represented by a different union, and therefore could not be cross-utilized.

In-House Expertise and Problem Solving. In addition to keeping the work force small and challenged, cross-utilization and rotation were expected to add the benefits of a de facto ongoing quality and efficiency review. Problems could be identified and solutions and new efficiency measures could be continually invented if people were familiar with all aspects of the business and motivated to take managementlike responsibility for improving their company. Rotavonni spent some time each month on board the planes or in the ground operations area meeting employees and customers to learn better ways of doing things.

Facilities. Eagle's administrative offices and employee facilities at Midwest City International Airport could best be described as spartan and strictly functional. Offices were shared, few had carpeting, all had metal desks and comfortable yet functional employee lounges.

Customer waiting areas and ticket counter facilities, recently refurbished, were attractive and compared favorably with other carriers' facilities.

Reservations. The reservations system was kept extremely simple, fast, and therefore inexpensive. There were no interline arrangements with other airlines for ticketing or baggage transfer. However, assistance was offered with hotel or auto reservations, which appealed to business travelers. Reservation calls could be handled quickly by hundreds of easily trained temporary workers in cities served by Eagle, using local WATS lines and simple equipment versus the standard computer terminals. Ticketing was also done by travel agents.

Meal Service. Meal service was elegant by airline standards and a source of continual compliments particularly from business travelers. Gourmet meals were served on china and wine was complimentary. This was one cost item that Rotavonni felt was worth the extra expense because it complemented the quality service offered by the cabin crew.

Employees

Rotavonni repeatedly told his managers that Eagle's employees and its policies were what made the company unique and successful. The employee dimension is the value added to the commodity. Many investors still do not fully appreciate this point, but high commitment and participation plus maximum flexibility and massive creative productivity are the most important strategies at Eagle Airways.

Structure and Policies

In the few years during which Eagle Airways moved from a set of ideas to an operating business, Eagle's managers took pains to design structures and develop policies consistent with the company's stated precepts and strategies. This resulted in an organization characterized by minimal hierarchy, rotation and cross-utilization, work teams, ownership, self-management, participation, compensation, selective hiring and recruitment, multipurpose training, and team building.

Minimal Hierarchy. Eagle's initial organizational structure consisted of only three formal levels of authority. At the top of the organization was the president/CEO and six managing officers, each of whom provided line as well as staff leadership for more than one of the twelve functional areas (see Exhibit 3-1 for a list of functions).

Reporting to and working closely with the managing officers were six general managers, each of whom provided day-to-day implementation and leadership in at least one functional area, as well as planning for and coordinating with other areas. Eagle's managing officers and general managers worked hard at exemplifying the company's philosophy. They worked in teams, rotated out of their specialties as much as possible to take on line work, filling in at a gate or on a flight. Several had gone through the full "in-flight" training required of customer service managers. They shared office furniture and phones. Rotavonni's office doubled as the all-purpose executive meeting room; if others were using it when he had an appointment, he would move down the hall and borrow someone else's empty space.

There were no executive assistants, secretaries, or support staff of any kind. The managers themselves assumed the activities that such staff would ordinarily perform. Individuals, teams, and committees did their own typing, which kept written communications to a minimum. Everyone answered his or her own phone. (Both practices were seen as promoting direct communication as well as saving money.)

Beyond the top twelve officers, all remaining full-time management employees were either flight managers, maintenance managers, or

EXHIBIT 3-1 Eagle Airways Organizational Structure

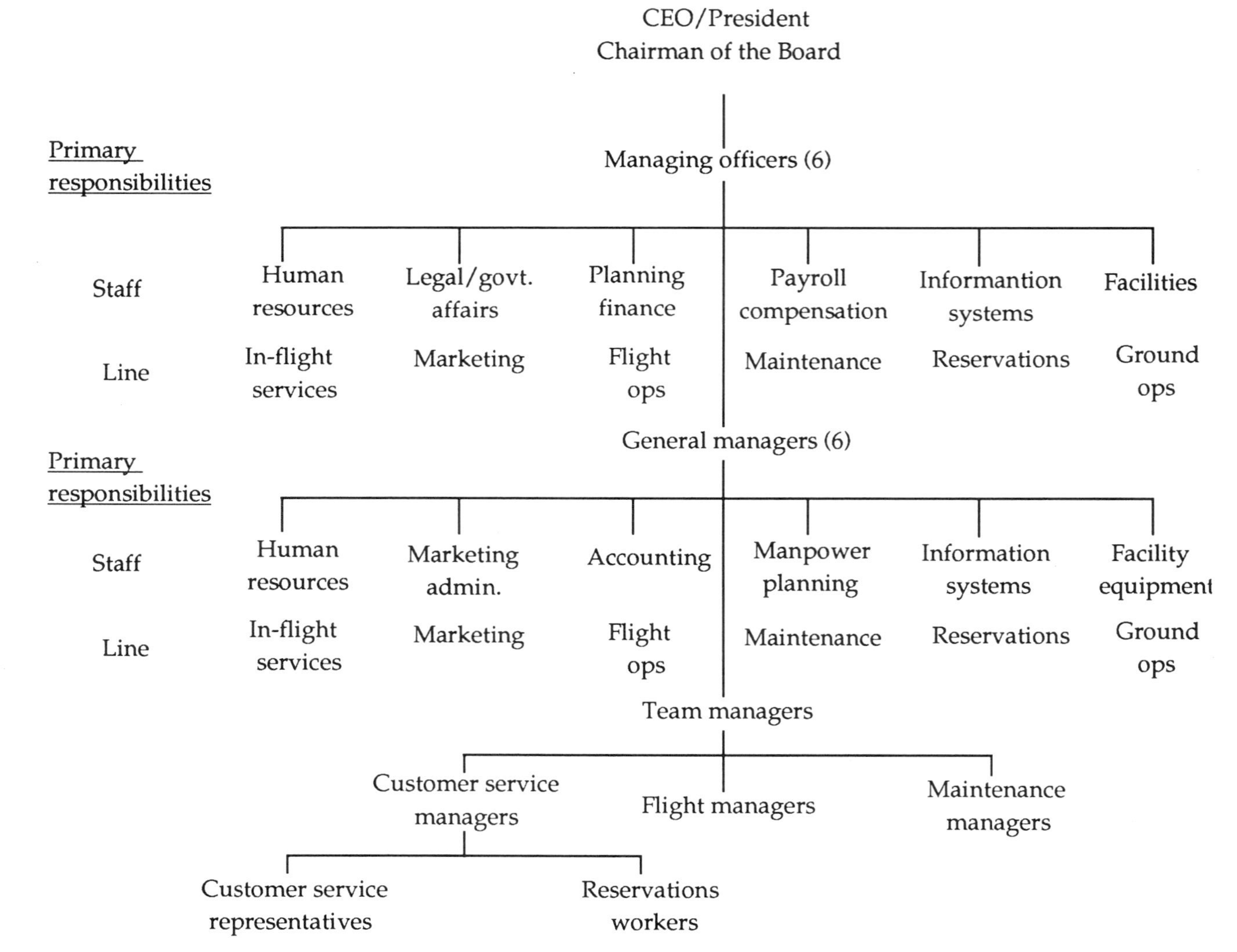

customer service managers. The titles indicated distinctions in qualifications and functional emphasis rather than organizational authority. Flight managers were pilots. Their primary responsibility was flying, but they also performed various other tasks, such as dispatching, scheduling, and safety checks, on a rotating basis or as needed. Maintenance managers were technicians who oversaw and facilitated maintenance of EA's airplanes, equipment, and facilities by contract with other airlines' maintenance crews. In addition to monitoring and assuring the quality of the contracted work, maintenance managers were utilized to perform various staff jobs.

The majority of Eagle's managers were customer service managers, generalists trained to perform all passenger-related tasks, such as security clearance, boarding, flight attending, ticketing, and food service, as well as some staff function activities. Customer service representatives and reservations workers, including many temporary full-time and part-time employees, reported to them.

The few authority distinctions that did exist were obscure and informal. Managing officers, general managers, and others with seniority (more than one year) had more responsibility for giving direction, motivating, teaching, and perhaps coordinating, but not for supervising or managing in the traditional sense.

Ownership and Job Security. Everyone in a permanent position at EA was a shareholder, required as a condition of employment to buy, at a greatly discounted price, a number of shares of common stock, determined on the basis of his or her salary level. It was expected that each employee, in keeping with being a manager/owner, would demonstrate a positive attitude toward work and participate in governing the company. A managing officer pointed out, "We'll fire someone only if it is absolutely necessary. . . . For instance, we won't tolerate dishonesty or willful disregard for the company's policies, but we don't punish people for making mistakes." In exchange, Eagle Airways promised the security of lifetime employment and opportunities for personal and professional growth through continuing education, cross-utilization, promotion from within the company, and compensation higher than other companies paid for similar skills and experience.

Cross-Utilization and Rotation. No one, regardless of work history, qualifications, or responsibility, was assigned to do the same job all the time. Everyone, including managing officers, was expected to be "cross-utilized" as needed and to rotate monthly between in-flight and ground operations and/or between line and staff functions.

Seen by some as unnecessarily complicated and troublesome, cross-utilization and rotation was justified by EA in several ways. According to Rotavonni, they were conceived primarily as methods of continuing education, aimed at keeping everyone interested, challenged, and growing. He appreciated the flexible staff utilization capability that eventually would result from everyone having broad exposure to the company's functions. Rotation did create some difficulties:

> It takes people a while to master each job. It might seem better to have an expert doing a given job. Cross-utilization also means you need high-quality people who are capable of doing several jobs. This in turn limits how fast you can recruit and how fast you can grow.

These were seen as short-term inconveniences well worth the long-term payoff:

> When you rotate people often they don't develop procedures that are too complicated for newcomers to learn and master fast. This forces the work to be broken down into short simple packets, easily taught and easily learned.

Self-Management. Employees were expected to manage themselves and their own work in collaboration with their teams and coworkers. According to the coordinator of training, "We don't want to teach behaviors—we want to teach what the end result should look like and allow each individual to arrive at those results in his or her own way. . . . When desired results aren't achieved, we try to guide people and assist them in improving the outcome of their efforts."

The written, though never formalized, guidelines regarding "self-management" read as follows:

> Within the context of our precepts and corporate objectives, and with leadership direction but no supervision, individuals and/or teams have the opportunity (and the obligation) to self-manage, which encompasses the following:
>
> - Setting specific, challenging, but realistic objectives within the organizational context.
> - Monitoring and assessing the quantity/quality/timeliness of one's own performance ("How am I doing?") by gathering data and seeking input from other people.
> - Inventing and executing activities to remedy performance problems and exploiting opportunities for improved performance.
> - Actively seeking the information, resources, and/or assistance needed to achieve the performance objectives.

When it came time for performance reviews, each individual distributed forms to those coworkers from whom feedback would be useful. Again, growth rather than policing was the objective.

Work Teams. Rotavonni observed that "even with smart, self-managed people, one person can't have all the components to be the answer to every situation." Eagle therefore had decided to organize its work force into small work groups (three or four people) as an alternative to larger groups with supervisors. "If you don't want a hierarchical structure with 40 levels you have to have some way to manage the numbers of people we were anticipating." Teams were seen as promoting better problem solving and decision making as well as personal growth and learning.

Every customer service manager belonged to a self-chosen ongoing team with which he or she was assigned work by a lottery system on a monthly basis. Though monthly staff assignments were made individually according to interests, skills, and needs, staff work was expected to be performed in teams. This applied to flight managers and maintenance managers as well as customer service managers. Each team was to elect a liaison to communicate with other teams. Each staff function was managed by a team of coordinators. Managing officers also worked in teams and rotated certain responsibilities to share the burden and the growth benefits of primary leadership.

Governance. Eagle's governance structure was designed with several objectives: policy development, problem solving, participation, and communications.

Although Rotavonni was the ultimate decision maker, top management decisions, including plans and policies, were to be made by management teams with the assistance of advisory councils. Each of the six managing officers and six general managers was responsible for at least one of the 12 functional areas (see Exhibit 3-1) and served on a management team for at least one other function. The 12 function-specific management teams were grouped into four umbrella staff committees: operations, human resources, marketing, and finance and administration. For each staff committee, composed of managing officers and general managers from the relevant functional areas, there was an advisory council made up of selected customer service managers, flight managers, and maintenance managers serving on relevant line and staff teams. The councils were intended to generate and review policy recommendations.

To minimize duplication and maximize communication, each advisory council elected a member to sit on an overarching "coordinating council" which was to meet regularly with Joe Rotavonni (to transmit information to and from him and among the councils). These ongoing teams and councils were supplemented periodically by ad hoc committees and task forces that could be created at anyone's suggestion to solve a particular problem, conduct a study, and/or develop proposals.

In addition to maximizing productivity, all of the above practices, teams, and committees were seen essential to promote personal growth and keep people interested in and challenged by their work.

High Compensation for Expected High Performance. Eagle's four-part compensation package was aimed at reinforcing its human resource strategy. Base salaries were determined strictly by job category on a relatively flat scale, ranging in 1989 from $28,000 for customer service managers to $60,000 for the managing officers and CEO. (Competitor airlines averaged only $20,000 for flight attendants after several years of service, but paid nearly double for managing officers and more than four times as much for their chief executives.)

Whereas most companies shared medical expenses with employees, Eagle paid 100% of all medical and dental expenses. Life insurance, rather than being pegged to salary level, was $75,000 for everyone.

After one year with EA, all managers' base salary and benefits were augmented by three forms of potential earnings tied to the company's fortunes. There were two profit-sharing plans, a dollar-for-dollar, based on quarterly profits and paid quarterly to full-time employees who had been with EA over one year, and a plan based on annual profitability. The former was allocated proportionally according to salary level and distributed incrementally. If profits were large, those at higher salary levels stood to receive larger bonuses, but only after all eligible managers had received some reward. The sustained profits were distributed annually and equal amounts to employees in all categories. Together, earnings from these plans could total up to 50 percent or more of base salary.

Finally, EA awarded several stock option bonuses, one nearly every quarter, making it possible for managers who had worked at least half a year to purchase limited quantities of common stock at discounts ranging form 25 to 40 percent of market value. The company offered five-year, interest-free promissory notes for the full amount of the stock purchase required of new employees, and for two-thirds the amount of any optional purchase.

Selective Hiring of the Eagle Airways "Type." Given the extent and diversity of responsibilities Eagle required of its employees, the managing officer in charge of the company's human resources as well as in-flight services believed firmly that it took a certain type of person to do well at Eagle Airways. Recruiters looked for people who were bright, educated, well groomed, mature, articulate, assertive, creative, energetic, conscientious, and hard working. While they had to be capable of functioning independently and taking initiative, and it was desirable for them to be ambitious in terms of personal development, achievements, and wealth, it was also essential that they be flexible, collaborative rather than competitive with coworkers, excellent team players, and comfortable with EA's horizontal structure. "If someone needed to be a vice president in order to be happy, we'd be concerned and might not hire them."

Recruiting efforts for customer service managers were pitched deliberately to service professionals—nurses, social workers, teachers—with an interest in innovative management. No attempt was made to attract those with airline experience or interest per se. Applicants who came from traditional airlines where "everyone memorized the union contract and knew you were only supposed to work *x* number of minutes and hours" were often ill-suited to Eagle's style. They were not comfortable with its loose structure and broadly defined, constantly changing job assignments. They were not as flexible as Eagle Airways types.

The flight manager positions were somewhat easier to fill. Many pilots from commuter and small regional carriers were anxious to move up to heavier equipment and higher pay. Eagle Airways had an abundant pool of applicants. All licensed pilots had already met certain intelligence and technical skill criteria, but not every qualified pilot was suited or even willing to be an Eagle Airways flight manager. Though flying time was strictly limited to the FAA's standard 30 hours per week (100/month, 1,000/year) and rules regarding pilot rest before flying were carefully followed, additional staff and management responsibilities could bring a flight manager's work week to anywhere from 50 to 70 hours.

Furthermore, FMs were expected to collaborate and share status with others, even nonpilots. In return for being flexible and egalitarian—traits that were typically somewhat in conflict with their previous training and job demands—pilots at EA were offered the opportunity to learn the business, diversify their skills and interests, and benefit from profit sharing and stock ownership, if and when the company succeeded.

Recruitment Process. Applicants for the position of CSM who qualified after two levels of tests and interview with recruiters were granted a "board interview" with at least one general manager and two other senior people who reviewed psychological profiles and character data. In a final review after a day-long orientation, selected candidates were invited to become trainees. One out of 100 CSM applicants was hired (see Exhibit 3-2 for a CSM profile).

In screening pilots, "the interview process was very stringent. Many people who were highly qualified were eliminated." Only one out of three flight manager applicants were hired.

Training and Team Building. The training program for CSMs lasted for five weeks, six days a week, without pay. At the end, candidates went through an in-flight emergency evacuation role-play and took exams for oral competency as well as written procedures. Those who tested at 90 or above were offered a position.

The training was designed to enable CSMs, many without airline

EXHIBIT 3-2 Eagle Airways—Profile of a Customer Service Manager

LOOK FOR CANDIDATES WHO:

1. Appear to pay special attention to personal grooming.
2. Are composed and free of tension.
3. Show self-confidence and self-assurance.
4. Express logically developed thoughts.
5. Ask intelligent questions; show good judgement.
6. Have goals; want to succeed and grow.
7. Have strong educational backgrounds; have substantial work experience, preferably in public contact.
8. Are very mature self-starters with outgoing personality.
9. Appear to have self-discipline; are good planners.
10. Are warm but assertive personalities, enthusiastic good listeners.

APPEARANCE GUIDELINES

Well-groomed, attractive appearance.

Clean, tastefully worn, appropriate clothing.

Manicured, clean nails.

Reasonably clear complexion.

Hair neatly styled and clean.

Weight strictly in proportion to height.

No offensive body odor.

Good posture.

Good teeth.

For women, makeup should be applied attractively and neatly.

Above listed guidelines apply to everyone regardless of ethnic background, race, religion, sex, or age.

experience, to perform multiple tasks and be knowledgeable about all aspects of an airline. Three full days were devoted to team building, aimed at developing trainees' self-awareness, communication skills, and sense of community. "We try to teach people to respect differences, to work effectively with others, to build synergy.'"

On the last team-building day everybody chose two or three others with whom to start work. These groups became work teams, Eagle's basic organizational unit. Initially, according to management, these decisions tended to be based on personalities and many trainees were reluctant to choose their own work teams. They were afraid of hurting people's feelings or being hurt. Trainers would remind them that Eagle Airways gave them more freedom than they would get in most companies, more than they were used to, and that "freedom has its price. . . It means you've got to be direct and you've got to take responsibility."

Over time, trainers learned to emphasize skills over personalities as the basis of team composition and to distinguish work teams from friendship groups. Choosing a work team became a business decision.

QUESTIONS

1. Do you feel that Eagle Airways, as a regional carrier, has taken the correct approach in providing exemplary service primarily directed at business travelers flying out of secondary hubs in the Midwest?

2. Discuss Rotavonni's organizational philosophy. How does it compare with traditional management theory?

3. Compare and contrast the organizational structure and policies of Eagle Airways with those of more traditional air carriers described in Chapter 7, *Air Transportation: A Management Perspective,* SecondEdition (Wadsworth, 1989). Discuss some of the pros and cons of Eagle's structure and policies for the short-term and long-term period.

Justification for the New Service
Chicago-Los Angeles Passenger Traffic
Analysis of Traffic by Trans-States

4
TRANS-STATES AIR LINES
Fare Options

In February 1989, management at Trans-States Air Lines (TS) debated the results of an experiment designed to measure the effects of a proposed "three-class" service on selected nonstop flights between Chicago and Los Angeles (ORD-LAX). Starting in August 1988, TS had advertised extensively that the existing two-fare service (consisting of first class and coach) would be replaced on certain flights with first, business, and economy classes. The new fares and service were limited to the ORD-LAX route on an experimental basis. Beginning in September 1988, three-class service was inaugurated with one-way fares set at $245 for first class, $185 for business, and $130 for economy. Other flights continued to operate on the old two-class basis with fares of $245 for first class and $175 for coach.

JUSTIFICATION FOR THE NEW SERVICE

Since deregulation, the percentage of total passenger miles traveled in coach on United States domestic air carriers had increased considerably. The percentage change was even higher on the ORD-LAX route. This movement to increased coach travel was caused by cost considerations in personal travel, as well as by increasing business requirements that expense account travel must be in coach rather than first class. According to Trans-States, the new service was "designed to broaden the air travel market more adequately, compensate the air line for the services provided, and prevent further transfer of business to lower cost services. . . . Present coach fares do not compensate the carrier fully for the services provided. . . . Trans-States' plan offers the way to a dramatic breakthrough that will benefit the public as much as the carrier."

Under the old two-class system, the main differences between first class and coach were:

First Class	*Coach*
6-abreast seating	7-abreast seating
Wider seats with 38 in. pitch	Coach seats with 34 in. pitch
Free beverages	Beverages sold
Deluxe food	Regular food
More luxurious cabin	

The differences in services offered on the new three-fare plan were:

First Class	*Business Class*
6-abreast seating	7-abreast seating
Wider seats with 38 in. pitch	Business class seats with 34 in. pitch

Free beverages	Free beverages
Deluxe food	Regular food
More luxurious cabin	

Economy

9-abreast seating

Coach seats with 32 in. pitch

Beverages sold

No meals

The operating costs per mile per available seat, whether occupied or not, for the various classes of service were estimated as follows:

Two-Class Service	
First class	\$0.082
Coach	0.048
Three-Class Service	
First class	\$0.082
Business class	0.056
Economy	0.039

(Airline distance between ORD and LAX is approximately 1,750 miles.)

Conversion to a three-class system permitted some increase in the number of seats per aircraft. Under the two-class system, a TS Boeing 767 had 18 first class seats and 198 coach seats. The same aircraft, operated on a three-class basis, had 18 first class seats, 70 business class seats, and 144 economy class seats.

CHICAGO-LOS ANGELES PASSENGER TRAFFIC

Following the initiation of the new three-class service by Trans-States, management from TS and its three competitors on this route studied the passenger traffic statistics closely to see the effect of the new service. Passenger traffic figures were derived from a 10 percent continuous sample of airline tickets compiled by the DOT.

There are two principal methods of measuring airline traffic: (1) origin and destination (O & D), including only those passengers traveling between two specific points with no connections at either end; and (2) on-board (OB), including *all* passengers on board an aircraft traveling from one point to another, including those continuing from connecting flights and those continuing beyond the terminus on either end.

Traffic statistics between ORD and LAX for the fourth quarter of 1987 and the entire year of 1988 are shown in Exhibit 4-1. Additional traffic statistics for the same period are shown in Exhibit 4-2.

The controversy over the statistics arose primarily over the question of how much of the increase in traffic during the fourth quarter of 1988 had been caused by the reduction in fares versus normal growth and diversion of customers from other routes and carriers. For example, a passenger might be diverted from a competing carrier or from a direct New York-Los Angeles flight to a New York-Chicago-Los Angeles route by the new fare structure and service. Trans-States recognized that *some* of the increase represented diversion and that some of it was "new" traffic generated by the three-class fare. There was sharp disagreement, however, on the relative importance of the "new traffic."

Estimation of the amount of "generated" traffic was a key question in appraising the results of the experiment. The loss of revenue suffered as a result of three coach passengers ($175 each) switching to economy ($130 each), which had to be offset by approximately one new economy class traveler. Hence, TS sought to determine how much of the traffic increase shown in Exhibit 4-1 should be attributed to normal growth, how much reflected diversion of passengers from other carriers or other routes in the absence of the economy fare, and how much was actually *new* traffic.

ANALYSIS OF TRAFFIC BY TRANS-STATES

One approach developed by Trans-States was a statistical analysis of the trends in passenger traffic for ORD-LAX and other routes during the period from the fourth quarter of 1987 through the fourth quarter of 1988. First, they compared increases in traffic between LAX and major eastern/midwestern cities (including Chicago) with increases in traffic (1) between LAX and nine cities not affected by economy fares and (2) for all domestic airline routes of 1,500 miles or more. They reasoned that, if the experimental fares had generated a significant amount of new traffic, the growth rates for LAX-Eastern and Midwestern cities should have been greater than the growth rates for the two "control groups" of routes. The traffic comparisons were as follows:

Fourth Quarter 1987 vs. 1988	*Los Angeles Midwestern and Eastern Markets* +14.3%
Nine Los Angeles Markets Not Affected by Economy Fares +14.8%	*All Domestic Markets of 1,500 Miles or More* +15.5%

EXHIBIT 4-1 Trans-States Air Lines Average Daily Passenger Traffic between Chicago and Los Angeles

Origin and Destination (O & D) and On-Board (OB) Passengers

		O & D Passengers Ave. Psgrs./day (One-wayTot. Mkt.)		Trans-States	On-Board Passengers Ave. Psgrs./day (One-wayTot. Mkt.)		Trans-States
Yr.	Qtr.	Total	Coach*	% of Total Mkt.	Total	Coach*	% of Total Mkt.
87	4	3,350	2,950	29 %	6,990	6,015	17 %
88	1	3,190	2,840	25	7,000	6,125	16
	2	3,600	3,275	22	7,720	6,795	13
	3	4,230	3,810	22	9,540	8,445	12
Test Began							
	4	4,640	4,360	23	9,330	8,675	13

*"Coach" passenger figures include regular coach, business, and economy class passengers during the 4th quarter of 1988.

EXHIBIT 4-2 Trans-States Air Lines Flights and Average Number of Seats Provided per Day between Chicago and Los Angeles

Yr.	Qtr.	Ave. Trips/day* (One-way TS)	Ave. Seats Provided/Day (One-way TS)	Percent of Seats Occupied (load factor)
87	4	14	2,900	75 %
88	1	12	2,700	71
	2	12	2,700	67
	3	13	2,850	73
Test Began				
	4	15	2,950	77

*Includes B-727, 747, and 767 equipment including originating and through trips.

A second type of statistical analysis was designed to provide estimates of the *share* of total Los Angeles passenger traffic going to cities affected by the economy fares. In this analysis, regression equations were developed to estimate the percentages of all traffic between Los Angeles/San Francisco and four groups of cities: (1) those affected by the economy fares; (2) other eastern/midwestern cities; (3) eight southern cities; and (4) nine other cities not affected by economy fares. The regression equations, based on traffic trends prior to the introduction of the new fares, indicated that in the absence of economy fares, the first group of cities would have been expected to account for 78.2 percent of the total traffic. The actual figure for the fourth quarter of 1988 was 78.5 percent.

On the basis of these and several other statistical analysis, it appeared to TS management that the three-class service and experimental fares had very little effect on total traffic between ORD and LAX.

On-Board Passenger Survey

Because the estimation of "generated" traffic was regarded as such an important problem, TS decided to conduct a survey of ORD-LAX passengers during the fall of 1988. The survey was conducted by placing questionnaires in the storage pockets facing each seat on the flights providing economy class service. Flight attendants encouraged passengers to complete the questionnaires and then collected the completed forms.

Responses to Question 6 in the questionnaire were used to estimate traffic generation. Question 6 asked: If economy class service were *not available,* which of the following would you have done about your trip today?

a. Would have flown coach class on another TS flight.

b. Would have flown coach class on another airline.

c. Would have gone by auto.

d. Would have taken the train or bus.

e. Would *not* have made this trip *at all.*

f. Other (Please specify).

Of all the ORD-LAX passengers who supplied answers during the four months beginning in September 1988, about 16 percent indicated that in the absence of economy fares, they would not have traveled by air. During September, October, and November, this represented about 12 percent of all ORD-LAX passengers.

Passenger Interview Survey

Because the results of the on-board passenger survey conflicted with the statistical analysis, TS retained a reputable market research organization to evaluate the experiment independently by means of a second questionnaire survey. The organization was to determine what fraction of the ORD-LAX economy class passengers would *not* have flown if economy class had not been available.

As a first step, the market research firm conducted a pilot study of 60 personal interviews in early January 1989 to determine the final questionnaire and sample design and to study procedures. The full-scale survey was then conducted in February 1989 in Chicago with persons who had flown economy class from ORD-LAX during the previous quarter. The research technique was to interview people at home or by telephone who had made economy class flights during the fourth quarter of 1989.

More than 350 interviews were conducted. All respondents were approached as part of an unidentified travel survey, and broad travel questions led indirectly to the respondent discussing his or her economy trip. In tabulating the answers, the research organization weighted the responses in accordance with the importance of each type of passenger in the total ORD-LAX traffic. Thus the sample was weighted so as to reflect the proper distribution of men versus women, business versus nonbusiness travelers, and early versus late reservations.

The key problem in interpreting the responses to the passenger interview survey was that of classifying each respondent as "generated" or "nongenerated." The research firm used both the *direct responses* to the questionnaire and *inferences based on patterns of responses* in classifying passengers into the two categories. Direct responses used in classifying passengers included the answers to the following questions:

12b. If the air fare had been about 35 percent more than it was, would you have made the trip?

Yes ____ No ____

19b. Suppose economy class, the class you flew, was sold out at the time you were making your reservation. Which of the following actions would you probably have taken? (Read list)

Rescheduled the trip to stay on economy class ____

Chosen coach class on another TS flight ____

Chosen coach class on another airline ____

Traveled to Chicago/Los Angeles some other way ____

Traveled somewhere else ____

Would not have taken the trip at that time ____

Don't have any idea ____

22a. As far as you know, has there been an air travel fare reduction between Chicago and Los Angeles in the past year or so?

Yes ____ No ____

b. Has this caused you to fly there more frequently?

Yes ____ No ____

Information used in making inferences about the passenger's probable behavior in the absence of economy fares included:

(A) The passenger's *awareness* of airline fares and of the economy fare in particular:

8b. What kind of information did you obtain from the airlines or a travel agent regarding fares before you decided to fly?

____

11. Which of the following considerations was *most* and *least* important to you in your decision to make your last trip by air? Comfort, Cost, On-time performance, Schedule availability, Carrier's image, Safety.

Most important ____________ Least important ____________

13a. Did you make your reservation direct or did someone else, such as a travel agent or company personnel, make it for you?

Respondent made reservation____

Someone else made reservation ____

b. If someone else made the reservation, what instructions did you give that person in order for them to make the reservation?

____

c. Did they find out anything for you about the fare before they made the reservation?

Yes ____ No ____

d. If yes, what was that? ______________________________

16. About how much was the fare on your flight between Chicago and Los Angeles?

____

17. What, approximately, do you think is the price difference or percentage difference between economy class and the next lowest price for a one-way flight for one person between Chicago and Los Angeles? $____________

18a. Did you discuss price differences between the various fare classes and carriers with airline or travel agency personnel or other people prior to choosing economy class?

Yes ____ No ____

b. Did you know about the economy class before you made the reservations?

Yes ____ No ____

(B) The extent to which alternative means of transportation were considered:

8a. When you made the decision to go to (Chicago/Los Angeles), what other methods of travel, if any, did you consider?

Train ____ Auto ____ Bus ____ None ____

(C) Whether the trip was for business or pleasure:

7a. Was your trip to (Chicago/Los Angeles) exclusively business, partially business, or exclusively nonbusiness?

Exclusively business ______

Partially business ______

Exclusively nonbusiness ______

b. If this trip was flown for business purposes, does your company have a policy regarding the fare class that you generally use when flying? Yes ____ No ____

c. If yes, what is the policy? ______________________

(D) The length of the trip:

4. How many days did you remain in (Chicago/Los Angeles)?

1 day	____	2 weeks	____
2–3 days	____	3–4 weeks	____
4–7 days	____	More than 1 month	____

Interviewers from the research firm utilized both direct and inferential information in determining whether or not a given passenger had been "generated" by the economy fare. Where the two types of information agreed, it was felt that considerable confidence could be placed in the result. Where they conflicted, the interpretation was made only after the interviewer's conclusion had been supported by an independent analysis made by another analyst in the research firm. In 92 percent of the cases, the interviewer and the analyst agreed on the classification.

Following this procedure for classifying passengers, the research firm concluded that 10 percent of the economy class passengers had been "generated" by the experimental fares and service. The detailed estimates were as follows:

	Overall Evaluation	*Evaluation by Interviewer*	*Analyst*
Were generated	10 %	12 %	15 %
Not generated	88	88	85
Undetermined	2	—	—

Estimates of traffic generation for various *types* of passengers are shown in Exhibit 4-3.

EXHIBIT 4-3 Estimates of Percentages of Economy Class Passengers Generated by Experimental Fares, by Types of Passengers(Based on Overall Evaluations of the Passenger Interview Survey)

Types of Passengers and Number in Group	Percent of Type Classified as Generated	Not Generated	Undetermined
All economy passengers (352)	10%	88%	2%
Passengers flying for:			
Exclusively business (130)	3	97	—
Partially business (53)	6	94	—
Nonbusiness (169)	13	84	3
Passengers who considered:			
No alternative modes of transportation (306)	8	90	2
At least one alternative (46)	19	78	3
Male passengers (187)	6	93	1
Female passengers (165)	15	83	2
Passengers with incomes:			
Under $15,000	19	74	7
$15,000–25,000	10	90	—
$25,000–50,000	11	85	4
Over $50,000	7	93	—

QUESTIONS

1. Discuss the pros and cons of the proposed three class service on selected Trans-States flights between ORD-LAX. Is this a better strategy than simply reserving a percentage of coach seats at a lower promotional fare? Determine the BE loadfactor for the two- and three-class services.

2. Do you see any problems with the statistical analysis of passenger traffic that TS completed? Why might the on-board passenger survey be a better indicator of the generative effect of lower fares?

3. Do you think it was necessary to conduct the passenger interview survey? Why?

4. Based on the statistical analysis, on-board survey, and interview survey, would you continue the three-class service?

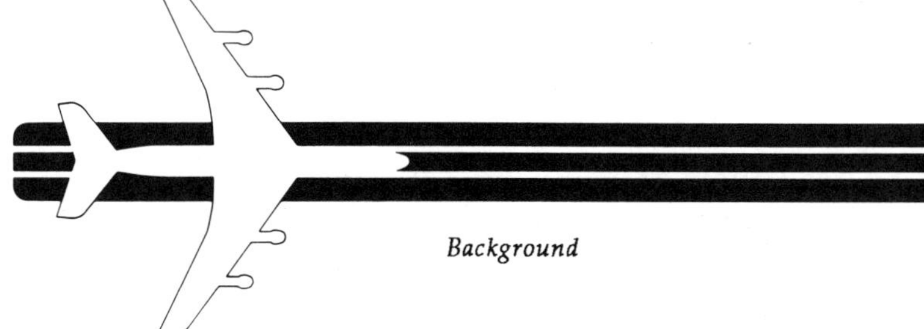

5

AIR SOUTH, INC.

Scheduling and Costs

BACKGROUND

A product of deregulation, Air South, Inc. (AS) is just regaining profitability in 1988 after three years of losses. (See Income Statement for 1987 in Exhibit 5-1.) During those three years AS entered many new markets that were of longer distance, higher density, and more competitive than those it had previously served. (See Exhibit 5-2 for Top 20 Markets.) Concurrently, it upgraded much of its jet fleet, acquiring 10 between 1982 and 1986. Management must now determine how to compete effectively in these new markets and how to position the airline through scheduling or other strategies to minimize its vulnerability to actions by competitors many times the size of this regional carrier.

In the 1987 annual report to stockholders, management stated:

> Efforts fall short of providing adequate jet service to all our potentially good markets. For example, in Oseola-Tropical City, our current five round trips daily are not adequate to meet demand created by tremendous growth in industry and tourism. In other markets, we are forced to offer only multistop service.
>
> Historically, traffic in our region has been controlled by a large major carrier whose strategy has been to consolidate all regional traffic in Metropolis and provide connections to other national cities. This has caused Metropolis to become one of the busiest of U.S. airports even though approximately 70 percent of the traffic represents connecting passengers. Metropolis is known for its holding delays on arrivals and departures. This creates a ripe opportunity to offer "bypass Metropolis" service throughout the region.

The company is now considering providing direct service between various points as an alternative to connecting flights through hubs. To fly from Robertsville (RBV), Tropical City (TPC), and Oseola (OSA) to Sheffieldsville (SFV), Olympus (OPS), or Fordsville (FDV) and from Robertsville (RBV) to St. Bart (STB), a passenger had to change planes in Metropolis (Met). The size of these markets is shown in Exhibit 5-3. Air South participated in the MET-OPS, SFV, and FDV legs only in a minor way, as shown in Exhibit 5-4, usually when the passenger had booked through AS.

The market share AS hoped to capture was a function of the relative number of flights offered and their convenience. Air South developed a measure called the Quality of Service Index (QSI), which reflected these factors. A simplified version of this technique is calculated by assigning points to each flight based on the type of service: 1.0 for nonstop to destination; 0.5 for one-stop; 0.3 for two-stop or nonstop connecting with nonstop; 0.1 for three-stop. The sum of these points over a city-pair is the QSI. A carrier's service share is computed as the ratio of its QSI to the total QSI in the market. For example, 6 flights/day are offered from

EXHIBIT 5-1 1987 Income Statement for Air South, Inc.

	($000)
Operating Revenue	
Passenger	$47,676
Mail, express, freight	5,390
Charter	6,367
Other	901
Total	$60,334
Operating Expenses	
Flying operations	$20,950
Maintenance	10,808
Aircraft and traffic servicing	13,523
Passenger service	3,314
Promotion and sales	4,774
General & administrative	3,921
Depreciation and amortization	2,617
Total	$59,927
Operating Income	407
Other deductions (income)	
Interest on long-term debt	845
Tax effect*	(326)
Net Income	(112)

* Includes income tax, tax loss carry forward, and investment tax credit.

EXHIBIT 5-2 AS Top 20 Markets, 1987

Market	Passengers AS	Passengers Tot. Market	AS Share	Competition*	Nonstop Mileage
WTY – OPS	47,600	280,000	17%	OG	486
MET – HTV	130,000	130,000	100%	None	151
MET – VPS	72,000	72,000	100%	None	250
MET – GPT	40,000	40,000	100%	None	352
MET – PEN	56,000	56,000	100%	None	247
TPC – TLH	35,640	66,000	54%	EC	403
MET – DHN	74,000	74,000	100%	None	171
ADI – VPS	16,000	16,000	100%	None	783
OPS – STB	49,920	156,000	32%	OG	256
ABY – MET	82,000	82,000	100%	None	146
CSG – GLA	12,900	30,000	43%	OG, EC, CO	831
OSA – TPC	50,760	188,000	27%	OG, EC, CO	196
CSG – ADI	15,200	20,000	76%	OG, EC, CO	619
GPT – OPS	20,000	20,000	100%	None	325
OPS – BOM	22,000	22,000	100%	None	317
MET – BOM	22,000	100,000	22%	EC	302
HTV – OPS	40,000	40,000	100%	None	185
SFV – OPS	33,600	40,000	84%	OG	211
OSA – TLH	30,000	30,000	100%	None	225
MET – MEI	24,480	36,000	68%	OG	267

* Competition: Omega (OG), East Coast (EC), Coastal (CO).

EXHIBIT 5-3 Existing as Markets 1988[a]

	Round-trip Passengers/year			
	Sheffieldsville (SFV)	*Olympus (OPS)*	*Fordsville (FDV)*	*St. Bart (STB)*
Robertsville (RBV)	18,000	19,000	15,000	20,000
Oseola (OSA)	26,000	30,000	12,000	25,000
Tropical City (TPC)	35,000	55,000	32,000	N/A

[a]All current service connects over Metropolis with six nonstop flights between each city and Metropolis. N/A (not applicable): nonviable segment (long-haul with major carriers).

EXHIBIT 5-4 As Share of Existing Traffic, 1988

Routing	Segment Offered by AS	AS Share Segment (%)	Annual AS R/T Revenue from Segment
RBV – SFV via MET	MET – SFV	8	$69,550
RBV – FDV via MET	MET – FDV	12	110,880
RBV – OPS via MET	MET – OPS	5	76,000
OSA – SFV via MET	MET – SFV	8	100,460
OSA – FDV via MET	MET – FDV	12	88,700
OSA – OPS via MET	MET – OPS	4	96,000
TPC – SFV via MET	MET – SFV	5	84,520
TPC – FDV via MET	MET – FDV	8	157,700
TPC – OPS via MET	MET – OPS	3	132,000

OSA to OPS connecting over MET with nonstop service on each leg. If AS offered 1 flight/day nonstop OSA-OPS, its anticipated service share would be 36 percent (competition: 6 flights/day x .3 pt./flight = QSI of 1.8; AS: 1 flight/day x 1.0 pt./flight = QSI of 1.0; service share = 1.0/2.8 = .36). This method was usually reliable within a 10 to 15 percent tolerance. In addition, experience showed that due to the creation of new gateways and more convenient travel patterns, the first direct nonstop service in a market had a stimulative effect of 10 percent, whereas the first direct one-stop service had a 5 percent stimulative effect. Air South identified seven possible bypass Metropolis aircraft itineraries. Exhibit 5-5 characterizes these itineraries and gives net per-passenger revenues for the associated segments. Competitors were offering six daily round trips connecting over MET in the nine markets connecting RBV, TPC, and OSA with SFV, OPS, and FDV and in RBV-STB. Other than those nine, markets associated with the proposed rotations, such as TPC-OSA, OPS-STB, and SFV-STB, were generally so large that a certain amount of traffic would accrue just because of a carrier's presence. Air South expected to board an average of 10 passengers per departure in these markets. However, two- and three-stop service from TPC and OSA to STB was deemed uncarriable due to

EXHIBIT 5-5 Proposed AS Itineraries

Proposed Itineraries	One-way Flight Time
1. TPC – OSA – SFV – FDV	2 hrs 30 min
2. TPC – OSA – OPS	2 hrs 20 min
3. TPC – SFV – OPS – STB	3 hrs 12 min
4. RBV – OPS – STB	2 hrs 18 min
5. RBV – SFV – OPS – STB	2 hrs 32 min
6. TPC – OPS	2 hrs
7. TPC – OSA – SFV – OPS – STB	3 hrs 27 min

Net One-way Revenue*

	RBV	*TPC*	*OSA*	*SFV*	*OPS*	*FDV*	*STB*
RBV		N/A	N/A	85.00	115.00	N/A	135.00
TPC			58.30	125.00	148.30	141.60	173.30
OSA				101.60	126.60	120.00	150.00
SFV					61.60	55.00	91.60
OPS						N/A	68.30
FDV							N/A
STB							

* Fares have been diluted (net tax) due to discount fares, joint fares, and travel agent commissions.
N/A (not applicable): no present service.

superior available service.

Exhibit 5-6 illustrates the QSI calculation for proposed Itinerary 1 in Exhibit 5-5. The first step of the analysis is to break down the itinerary into component origin-destination combinations. Next, the QSI for the existing service is calculated for each segment. The QSI for the proposed additional AS service is calculated and the resulting AS share of the total QSI is multiplied by the existing market and any adjustments from stimulation due to new service. The expected AS revenue is then calculated for the proposed itinerary. The diversion from existing AS flights serving segments of these trips shown in Exhibit 5-4 must be deducted. This operation gives a net increase in revenue expected from the new itinerary. Exhibit 5-7 shows the results of a series of calculations of the type illustrated in Exhibit 5-5. All but Itinerary 4 show a positive contribution. However, more than the independent revenues and costs must be considered to determine the true profitability and feasibility of these itineraries. A more accurate comparison of flight itineraries might be made by computing contribution per flight hour.

Direct operating cost per hour was $1,600 based on nine and a half hours daily utilization. This amount included approximately 85 percent operating expenses except fixed overhead such as promotion, sales, and general and administrative expense, plus an allocation for ownership, which included depreciation and interest. The proposed itineraries must allow the planes to be scheduled at the fleet average of $1,600 per hour.

EXHIBIT 5-6 Sample QSI and Revenue Calculation for Aircraft Itinerary 1

Market	QSI Current Service Level	QSI Proposed Add'l. Service	AS Share of Market	Market Size. Rnd. Trip Pax/Year	AS Base Pax	Stimulation Factor	Tot. Rnd Trip Pax/ Year	Rev. per Pax ($)	Gross Revenue ($)
TPC-OSA	a						7,300	58.30	$ 425,590
TPC-SFV	1.8	.5	22%	35,000	7,700	5%	8,085	125.00	1,010,625
TPC-FDV	1.8	.3	14	32,000	4,480	0	4,480	141.60	634,368
OSA-SFV	1.8	1.0	36	26,000	9,360	10	10,296	101.60	1,046,074
OSA-FDV	1.8	.5	22	12,000	2,640	5	2,772	120.00	332,640
SFV-FDV	a						7,300	55.00	401,500
Total									$3,850,797

Diversions from Current Segments

Market	AS Segment	AS Revenue	
TPC – SFV	MET – SFV	$84,520	
TPC – FDV	MET – FDV	157,700	
OSA – SFV	MET – OSA	100,460	
OSA – FDV	MET – FDV	88,700	$ 431,380
Net Revenue			$3,419,417

[a]Incidental market producing 7,300 PAX/year round-trip.

EXHIBIT 5-7 Estimated Results of Adding Proposed Itineraries

Proposed Itinerary	Net Rev./Year	Direct Op. Cost/Year	Contribution per Year
1	$3,419,417	$2,920,000	$499,417
2	3,585,750	2,725,332	860,418
3	5,019,080	3,737,600	1,281,480
4	2,273,350	2,686,400	(413,050)
5	3,567,514	2,958,932	608,582
6	3,097,974	2,336,000	761,974
7	5,707,506	4,029,600	1,677,906

QUESTIONS

1. Using the time shown in Exhibit 5-5, determine the annual round-trip contribution per flight hour.

Itinerary	R/T hrs.	\$ per Flt Hour	Rank	\$ per Itinerary	Rank
1	______	__________	____	__________	____
2	______	__________	____	__________	____
3	______	__________	____	__________	____
4	______	__________	____	__________	____
5	______	__________	____	__________	____
6	______	__________	____	__________	____
7	______	__________	____	__________	____

2. Determine the annual direct operating costs (DOC) using the following formula:

DOC/yr = .85 (operating expenses – promotion and sales – general and administrative + 1,678)

DOC/yr = .85 (______ – ______ – ______ + 1,678) = $______

3. Determine the annual fully allocated cost (FAC) per hour using the following formula:

$$\text{FAC/hr.} = \frac{\text{DOC/hr x (operating expenses + interest)}}{\text{DOC/yr.}}$$

FAC/hr. = $______ x (__________ + __________) = $______

____

4. Determine the break-even load factor (BELF) based on DOC and FAC: (Compute the average BELF for each itinerary by multiplying the flight time by the cost, DOC or FAC, per hour and dividing by the revenue. There is a total of 60 seats on these aircraft.)

DOC ($ __________ /hr.)

	First to Last Point	Through Fare ($)	Flight Time (hrs)	Cost ($)	BE# PAX	BELF (%)
1.		$		$		
2.		$		$		
3.		$		$		
4.		$		$		
5.		$		$		
6.		$		$		
7.		$		$		

FAC ($ __________ /hr.)

1.		$		$		
2.		$		$		
3.		$		$		
4.		$		$		
5.		$		$		
6.		$		$		
7.		$		$		

5. Using the seven proposed itineraries, draw lines attaching each of the cities to give a visual impression of key cities and city pairs. Does this diagram give any hint of the strategic evolution of AS's system?

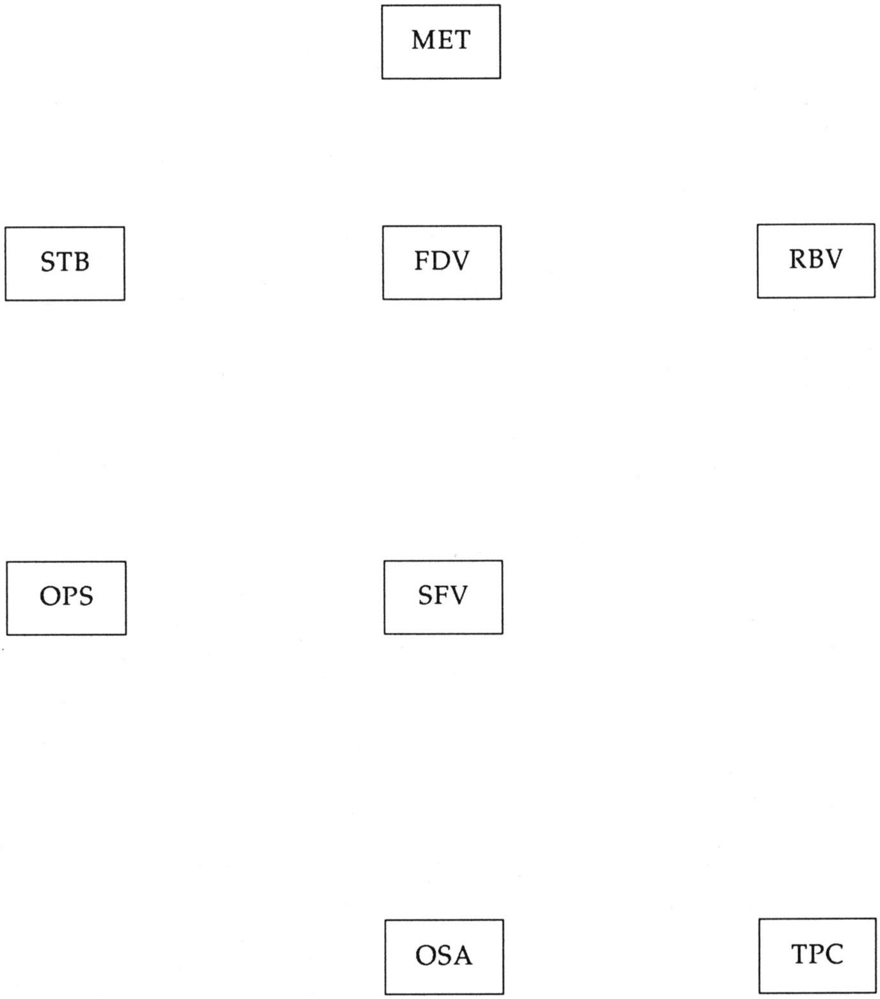

MET

STB FDV RBV

OPS SFV

OSA TPC

6. What do you think the competitive response from Omega (OG) will be, particularly in the OPS-STB, OSA-TPC, and SFV-OPS markets?

7. List the major factors carriers must consider in choosing among itineraries.

Introduction
Marketing Research
Marketing Strategy
Advertising Strategy

6
EASTERN AIR SERVICE
Expansion into New Markets

INTRODUCTION

Eastern States Air Service (ES) began service to several eastern cities in 1981 with three Boeing 737-200 aircraft and a marketing strategy that highlighted several unique approaches:

1. Simplicity of operations (one type of aircraft, simplified passenger check-in and fare structure, and no food service).
2. High productivity (daily aircraft utilization of more than 11 hours and 10 minutes turnaround time between most flights).
3. Focus on passenger business (no large air freight and no U.S. mail).
4. Serving short-haul, mass transit commuter markets (flight segments under two hours and a fare structure competitive with bus and auto travel).

By the end of March 1990, Eastern States Air Service had grown to 1,600 employees, 41 aircraft including F-28s and F-100s, 1,852 total system-wide weekly flights, and an average load factor of 68.3 percent (based on 1989 figures and a 94-seat capacity). Exhibit 6-1 illustrates the growth in passenger boardings over the years in operation, and Exhibits 6-2 and 6-3 give the firm's balance sheet and operating income at the end of the first quarter in 1989 and 1990.

Between 1982 and 1989, passengers carried grew at an annual rate of 48.9 percent. The reason for this growth, according to Eastern States' management, was that the carrier offered a good product and service in a receptive market at a fair price the average person could afford.

By the fall of 1988 ES served 11 eastern cities as a regional carrier. It prepared to inaugurate its first service out of the northeast into the south during the early part of the second quarter, 1990. The industry was entering a period of stabilization after the hectic 1980s with its new entrants, fare wars, bankruptcies, and mergers. The timing seemed right and Eastern States' business philosophy pointed to three cities with apparent growth potential: Leesberg, Coal City, and Great Smokeyville. Management felt that expanding air service to these cities from ES's Capital International Airport headquarters would be a profitable strategy.

MARKETING RESEARCH

The potential for expanding service appeared profitable, given the trends evident in 1989, total passenger boardings, load factors, and the projected growth. To supplement these data, however, a research project was conducted in the fall of 1989. A random, systemwide survey of

EXHIBIT 6-1 Eastern States Air Service Passenger Boardings

Year	Passenger Boardings
1981	108,554
1982	308,999
1983	543,407
1984	759,721
1985	1,136,318
1986	1,539,113
1987	2,339,524
1988	3,528,105
1989	5,000,086

EXHIBIT 6-2
Eastern States Air Service Consolidated Balance Sheet (in thousands) as of March 31

	1990	1989
Assets		
Current:		
Cash and commercial paper	$8,936	$8,374
Accounts receivable	11,678	5,447
Other	1,590	1,058
	22,204	14,879
Flight and ground equipment, at cost, less reserves	169,507	112,763
Other noncurrent assets	877	366
Total assets	$192,588	$128,008
Net Worth		
Common stock and paid-in capital	15,828	14,448
Retained earnings	47,810	31,488
Total net worth	63,638	45,936
Total liabilities and net worth	$192,588	$128,008
Liabilities		
Current:		
Accounts payable and accrued liabilities	$10,615	$6,287
Current maturities of long-term debt	4,720	1,750
	15,335	8,037
Long-term debt less current maturities	98,487	63,250
Deferred federal income tax	14,186	10,398
Deferred other	942	387
Total liabilities	128,950	82,072
Share Data		
Common stock issued and outstanding (000)	4,567	4,500
Book value per share	$13.94	$10.21

EXHIBIT 6-3 Eastern States Air Service Consolidated Statement of Income (in thousands) as of March 31

	1990	1989
Operating revenues:		
Passenger	$38,878	$24,732
Package express	1,116	799
Other	192	146
Total operating revenues	40,186	25,677
Operating expenses:		
Flight operations excluding fuel	3,470	2,453
Fuel and oil	12,631	5,286
Maintenance	2,383	1,521
Passenger services	1,654	1,173
Terminal operations	4,485	3,126
Promotion and sales	1,808	1,479
Insurance, taxes, and administrative	2,662	1,895
Depreciation	2,638	1,858
Employee profit sharing expense	923	688
Total operating expense	32,654	19,479
Operating Income	7,532	6,198
Nonoperating expense (income):		
Interest and other income	(1,020)	(40)
Interest expense	2,459	1,813
	1,439	1,773
Income before federal income tax	6,093	4,425
Provision for federal income tax	1,784	1,097
Net income	$4,309	$3,328
Weighted average common and common equivalent shares outstanding (000)	4,544	4,500
Net income per share	$ .95	$ .74

7,900 ES passengers was conducted on board flights to identify the frequency of flying and the attributes deemed important by these passengers.

Respondents were asked how many round-trip flights they had taken on Eastern States during the past year. The results (shown below) indicated that 18.7 percent of the respondents accounted for 55 percent of the total trips.

#of Flights	% Respondents	% Trips
1–2	22.9%	3 %
3–6	29.0	11
7–12	16.7	13
13–20	12.7	18
21–40	10.9	28
41+	7.8	27
	100.0%	100%

Respondents were also asked to evaluate various airline attributes in terms of importance, using a four-point rating scale (4 = very important; 1 = not important at all). As shown below, departing on time was rated as the most important attribute by the majority of those surveyed.

Attribute	Rank	% Respondents Rating Important
On-time departure	1	98.61%
Frequency of scheduled departures	2	97.86
Friendly ground personnel	3	97.12
Convenient departure times	4	96.99
Courteous flight attendants	5	95.51
Efficient baggage handling	6	93.0
Low fares	7	91.05

Respondents were also asked to indicate their particular likes and dislikes concerning Eastern States Air Service. Low fares was the highest ranked positive attribute.

Attribute	Rank
Low fares	1
Pleasant flight attendants	2
Convenient (in general)	3
On-time departure	4
Frequency of scheduled departures	5
Prompt and efficient service	6

MARKETING STRATEGY

Besides maintaining a consistent growth pattern on previously established routes, Eastern States' management's highest priority in 1990 was the introduction of the new routes to Leesberg, Coal City, and Great Smokeyville on April 1, 2, and 3 respectively. Service from Capital International Airport to these new markets was established as follows:

Market	Schedule
Leesberg	7 round-trips daily
Coal City	7 round-trips daily
Great Smokeyville	4–5 round-trips daily

Passengers arriving from these cities to Capital International Airport could connect with flights to the rest of Eastern States' system from Capital Airport. Similarly, passengers from other destinations could travel to these new cities through a connection at Capital Airport. However, ES did not plan to have any direct flights from the new cities to other Eastern States' markets until passenger load factors to Capital Airport were deemed successful.

To assist in the planning and development of these new routes, ES obtained a traffic history analysis of the 1988 origins and destinations (O & D) from each of the new markets. Capital International Airport was in the top four O & D cities from each of the new markets. Each of the cities had a population in excess of 500,000 and Coal City was just under 1 million.

Leesberg was the largest municipality in its state, representing the area's financial, commercial, and industrial center. Built on a rich farm base, the city now enjoyed a diversified economy including clothing manufacturing, food products, and electronics. A frequent convention center, Leesberg offered a variety of tourist attractions. It is located approximately 400 air miles from Capital Airport. Coal City was built on its steel and allied industries, which experienced difficult times during the 1970s but steadily rebounded after the recession in the early 1980s. During the past 10 years, it attracted a wide variety of light industry and its future looked particularly bright. The city was also home to several large universities that had successfully attracted research funding. A large Air Force base and related military suppliers were located near the city. Coal City is approximately 540 air miles from Capital International Airport. Great Smokeyville is a fast growing center of trade, light industry, and recreational opportunities. Its ski resorts had gained considerable popularity in recent years. A beautiful city of parks and old homes, Great Smokeyville recently attracted a number of federal projects including a major dam and hydroelectric facility. It is approximately 380 air miles from Capital Airport.

ADVERTISING STRATEGY

The introduction of the new routes was supported by a heavy radio and newspaper advertising campaign. Two weeks before the inaugural flights publicity releases were submitted to the media and small "teaser" advertisements were placed in the new market newspapers. The advertisements contained headlines such as "Eastern States Air Service Spreading Its Wings," and listed a phone number to make reservations.

That same week also began 60-second radio spots, running primarily in the morning and late afternoon, designed to reach businesspeople during drive time. ES's marketing team and its advertising agency felt that businesspeople represented the heaviest travelers and the appropriate target audience for these messages.

The week before the initial flights, the newspaper advertisements were stepped up to twice daily and the radio schedule was doubled. Nearly every radio station in the new markets was running Eastern States' spots. On March 29th, just days before the inaugural flights, full-page advertisements appeared in addition to the teaser newspaper advertisements in each of the local markets.

March 29th also marked the posting of 30-sheet billboards with messages such as "The Smart Shopper's Airline" and "Capital City, Little $" on major arterials throughout the new market cities. The full-page advertisements ran once daily through each inaugural flight, and radio stations broadcast "Capital City, Eastern States Style."

One month following the inaugural flights a marketing research study was performed to determine the effectiveness of the advertising campaign in each of the three cities. The survey questionnaire completed by passengers included the following questions:

1. Where do you recall seeing or hearing the Eastern States Air Service advertising of the new route service? (newspaper, radio, TV, billboard, magazine, don't know, and other)
2. In which newspaper(s) did you see this advertising? (local newspaper)
3. On which radio station(s) do you recall hearing this advertising? (local radio stations)
4. On which television station(s) do you recall seeing this advertising? (local and network TV stations)
5. Do you recall seeing or hearing news coverage about the new routes? Where? (newspapers, radio, TV, magazine)

6. Did you hear about the new route service from a travel agency? (yes or no)
7. What in the advertising attracted you? (convenience of Eastern States' schedule, low fares, high frequency of flights, friendly service)
8. What is your occupation? (professional, technical, manager, administrator, sales personnel, craftsmen, service worker, student, military, retired, unemployed)
9. Into which of the following age categories do you fall? (18–24, 25–34, 35–44, 45–54, 55–64, 65 and over)
10. Into which of the following categories does your total yearly household income fall? ($20,000 and under, $20,000–29,999, $30,000–39,999, $40,000–49,999, $50,000 and over)
11. How frequently do you fly? (once a week or more, two or three times a month, seldom)

In answer to the first question, newspapers ranked first by almost two to one over the next media, radio. Most passengers recalled seeing news coverage about the new routes in newspapers. By an overwhelming margin, passengers had not heard about the new route service from a travel agency. Passengers were attracted to the advertising by the convenience of Eastern States' schedule and low fares in about the same proportion. The great majority of passengers fell into the professional/technical and manager/administrator category covering the age groups from 25 to 54 with the 35–44 age group leading. The leading income group was from $30,000 to $39,999 with $40,000–49,999 following close behind. Most passengers flew two or three times a month.

QUESTIONS

1. What do consumers look for in selecting an airline? How important are these factors to the different market segments?

2. Why is price promotion so prevalent in the airline industry? Why do you think that low fares was the highest ranked positive attribute to Eastern States Air Service?

3. As a relatively new regional carrier attempting to make its first probe into new territory, what is the marketing task facing Eastern States Air Service?

4. Does Eastern States Air Service have any unique advantages as a regional carrier that the major and national carriers cannot match?

Background
The Scheduling Process
Competition

7
CONSTITUTIONAL AIRLINES
Scheduling and Fleet Operations

BACKGROUND

Constitutional Airlines (CT) is a large carrier with an extensive route structure throughout the United States. By December 1988, Constitutional's jet fleet included the following aircraft:

		Number of Seats per Aircraft (basic configuration)
70	B-727	180
62	B-737	115
9	B-747	330
18	B-757	178
8	B-767	211

The average airspeed for these jets (block to block) was 575 miles per hour.[1]

Constitutional was recovering from financial difficulties experienced during 1985–1986. Reported profits through November 1988 had increased some $20 million over the same period in the previous year, and with a good showing in December 1988 the airline hoped to earn $25 million on total revenues of approximately $1.5 billion. Crucial to this improvement was the upsurge in revenue passenger miles (RPMs) experienced during the latter part of 1987 and continuing into 1988. This increase in traffic was expected in light of the improved condition of the national economy during this period. The company had been built on a substantial volume of business travel. However, it was very aware of the importance of customers who travel for pleasure or personal reasons.

Constitutional's improved performance during the period of 1985 through 1987 resulted in cost cutting and overall "belt tightening" by the company. The management allowed attrition to reduce the level of the work force in nearly every classification. Because flight crews' salaries represent a significant cost item, CT was particularly conscious of the aggregate number of pilots it employed at any one time. Consequently, the company tried to hire and train additional pilots only after careful analysis of the flight schedule indicated that an increase was necessary. Normally, the time required to hire, train, and fit an experienced pilot into CT's schedule was about six weeks. Variations depended on the type of aircraft the pilot was being trained to fly as well

[1] Block-to-block time refers to the time when an aircraft begins to taxi until the time it arrives at its destination terminal. A jet's ground speed (actual speed over the ground) usually exceeds 600 mph.

as the availability of flight simulators, instructors, and training aircraft. Until July 1988, CT had not hired any new pilots for almost two years. As a result, their total number of "line pilots" had been reduced to approximately 3,700. During July and August, the airline hired 150 pilots in preparation for the increased activity forecast through 1989. Most of these pilots had recently begun flying as second officers aboard the company' B-727s.

Constitutional's Relations with Its Pilots

Like those of most of the larger airlines, Constitutional's pilots were represented in all wage and contract negotiations by the Air Line Pilots Association (ALPA). During the last 20 years this organization had been successful in improving the hours, pay, and working conditions of their pilots. For example, in 1968 a senior captain could earn around $60,000 annually and by 1988 this figure reached $90,000.

Under the terms of the contract in 1988, CT's pilots could fly a maximum of 80 "pay hours" per month. Pay hours referred not only to a pilot's actual flying time (block to block) but also included a portion of the time spent briefing and preparing for a flight as well as time traveling to or from a flight. For example, if a pilot based in Chicago were scheduled to take a flight from Chicago to New York to Atlanta and terminate in Miami, the pay hours would include all the flight time as well as a portion of the time required to fly the pilot from Miami to Chicago. Similarly, if the flight originated in Atlanta, part of the pilot's time traveling as a passenger from Chicago to Atlanta would count toward the 80 hours. For any month this scheduled "dead head" or credit time averaged approximately 20 percent of a pilot's actual pay hours.

Constitutional's Bidding System

Constitutional's pilots were usually qualified to operate only one type of aircraft, so substitutions of aircraft on a flight (say a B-737 series aircraft for a B-727 series aircraft) necessitated a change in flight crew. This was the result of the company's bid system covered under the ALPA contract. Under this system pilots could bid twice a year for the domicile (or base point) location and type of aircraft within CT's fleet that they would fly. The results of this bidding were determined by a pilot's seniority within his or her classification: captain, first officer, or second officer. One of each was required in the B-727 and B-747 aircraft. The other aircraft in CT's fleet were flown by a two-person crew. The most senior captain necessarily received his or her first choice as to base location and type of aircraft. This was true also for the most senior first officer and the most senior second officer. However, when a pilot advanced in classification, his or her seniority for bidding purposes was reduced.

When a pilot was assigned to a new type of aircraft, the Federal Aviation Administration (FAA) as well as CT required him or her to undertake simulated and actual flight training in that aircraft. This occurred prior to the pilot's first flight carrying passengers. Thus, after every bid, a certain number of CT's pilots were taken off the line and put through this training on the company's time. Normally the time required for this training was six to seven weeks, but it was usually spread out among the pilots so as not to interrupt the current flight schedule. Because of the seasonality of CT's operations, bids were conducted so that all training would be completed prior to June 1 and December 1 of each year. This enabled maximum utilization of pilots during the peak periods in CT's schedule. Once the date for a bid passed and a pilot was trained in the new aircraft, under the terms of the contract he or she could not fly any other aircraft, even though qualified to do so.

THE SCHEDULING PROCESS

As a large passenger carrier, CT's flight scheduling was an immensely complicated task. The airline had to look at the feasibility of serving any particular city pair within the context of the entire system. It was not enough to know that development of a certain market share on a route would yield a lucrative return. Alternative uses of aircraft and flight crews had to be considered along with the possible reaction of CT's competitors. Consequently, new ways were constantly being sought to improve CT's level of service in a way that would complement the existing operations.

A perfect schedule is rarely, if ever, attainable. The varied requirements, many of which are inherently in conflict with one another, simply cannot be satisfied simultaneously. For example, the schedule planner must endeavor to provide adequate ground time for servicing and maintenance and at the same time keep aircraft in the air for economic utilization. Departure times must be provided that are compatible with known customer preference, or complexes of connecting flights must be built at major gateways, at the same time avoiding excessive peaking of station activity. The planner must strive for schedule stability for the convenience of both passengers and employees, and at the same time rapidly adjust to new competitive threats or other developments. Public service obligations will sometimes work in the opposite direction from strictly economic considerations, yet the airline could not provide any service at all without a sound financial position (see Chapter 11, *Air Transportation: A Management Perspective*, Second Edition (Wadsworth, 1989)).

In short, when attempting to optimize the allocation of the airline's principal assets—its aircraft, facilities, personnel, and selling resources—and considering its route opportunities as well as its route obligations, the resulting patterns must meet the combined goals of public service, competitive effectiveness, operational performance, and profitability. During much of the process there is very little black or white but a great deal of gray. There is considerable coordination and, in fact, required inputs from each of the involved departments. It is the schedule planner's job to accomplish as many of the justifiable requests as possible.

Normally, CT's schedule of flights was written for a year in advance and updated quarterly as passenger forecasts and competitors' schedules changed. This schedule was then used by CT's marketing, flight ops, and maintenance administrations to plan for the delivery and utilization of different types of aircraft and the hiring, training, and scheduling of air crews and flight attendants. In the short run, however, the realities of the airline industry often dictated that this order be reversed. At any time, there was very little flexibility in aircraft and crew availability, and any unexpected change in the condition of one of these factors usually required some alteration of CT's flight schedule. For example, if a B-727 scheduled to fly from New York to Omaha experienced maintenance problems, the company might have another B-727 assigned as a backup in New York. If so, the substitution was made and the original aircraft would become a reserve when the repair work was completed. However, if a reserve aircraft was not available in New York, CT could either cancel the flight entirely or delay operations until another reserve aircraft could be flown in from another city. This necessitated breaking out another crew of pilots to fly the reserve aircraft into New York where they would either fly that aircraft to Omaha or turn it over to the original crew and "dead head" to their next assignment.

Scheduling for the Winter Months

Constitutional typically scheduled additional capacity during the latter half of December because of the high demand for travel during the Christmas holidays. The impact of this can be seen in the daily available seat miles offered in 1988 in Exhibit 7-1.

Although there was always some increase in activity in December and CT expected that, it was preferable to fall short of available pilot hours at this peak point of the annual operations rather than carry an excess number of pilots during slack periods. However, this year the situation was worse than normal. ALPA invoked a clause of the contract that required CT to place more pilots into training than had been predicted. This prevented these pilots from being used in December. Compounding these difficulties was the fact that delivery of CT's new B-747 aircraft was running significantly behind schedule. The company had hoped to use these aircraft in December and the allocation of crews had been set based on this expectation. This resulted in not only losing these large-capacity aircraft (330 seats each) but also tying up pilots from other

EXHIBIT 7-1 Forecasted ASM's, RPM's, and Load Factor for CT, December 1988

Date	Day	ASMs* (000)	RPMs** (000)	Load Factor %
1	R	73	48	65.7
2	F	73	49	67.1
3	S	74	44	59.5
4	S	74	46	62.2
5	M	72	44	61.1
6	T	70	40	57.1
7	W	71	40	56.3
8	R	72	45	62.5
9	F	73	51	69.8
10	S	74	39	52.7
11	S	74	48	64.8
12	M	72	44	61.1
13	T	70	39	55.7
14	W	86	43	50.0
15	R	89	50	56.2
16	F	90	59	65.6
17	S	89	55	61.8
18	S	92	49	53.3
19	M	91	48	52.7
20	T	92	53	57.6
21	W	93	67	72.0
22	R	93	75	80.6
23	F	93	78	83.9
24	S	93	65	69.9
25	S	90	56	62.2
26	M	89	61	68.5
27	T	90	72	80.0
28	W	88	63	71.6
29	R	89	65	73.0
30	F	90	57	63.3
31	S	92	67	72.8
Total		2,571	1,660	64.6

*ASM: available seat mile is a common measure for capacity in the airline industry. Technically, one ASM represents one aircraft seat traveling a distance of one mile.
**RPM: revenue passenger mile represents one aircraft seat (with a paying passenger) traveling a distance of one mile.

assignments under the terms of the ALPA contract.

The flight operations administration had experienced difficulty in meeting the November schedule. Because of these factors and extremely inclement weather, CT had exhausted all available monthly pilot hours in the B-727 and B-737 aircraft categories. Consequently, it was forced to cancel 40 flight segments between November 28 and 30. Of the 1,828 passengers scheduled on those flights CT had been able to satisfactorily reschedule 275 passengers on another CT flight; 974 were rescheduled on other carriers, while 579 were left "unprotected." Unprotected in this context meant that CT was unable to reschedule a passenger from a canceled flight on another flight to the original destination that arrived within two hours of the original arrival time. Because these November cancellations had all come during the last three days of the month, the percentage of passengers rescheduled on another CT flight was an extremely low 15 percent. Flight operations thought that, had they been able to selectively cancel the same amount of flights, they could have rescheduled approximately 50 percent of those passengers inconvenienced on Constitutional.

In actuality, the situation was worse than indicated. To complete a number of flights during the last two weeks of November, flight operations had scheduled some supervisory and instructor pilots on regular CT flights. Although these crews were fully qualified to operate aircraft, they were not considered line pilots under the terms of the ALPA contract. Thus, they could be scheduled for flights but they could not take flight time or pay hours from the regularly scheduled line pilots. Whatever flight time they accumulated in a line capacity had to be credited to a line pilot's record for scheduling and pay purposes. Since most pilots had used up their allowed 80 hours for November, this time was then credited on their records for December. The result was that CT started the month of December with some pilot pay hours already expended.

Flight Operations Reports

Constitutional made weekly projections of the total pilot hours (block hours and pay hours) required to operate the flight schedule for a particular month. Current records were also kept of the maximum available pilot capacity for the month. These figures were then compared to give an indication of the leeway, or cushion, existing in this area. So long as the aggregate number of available pay hours for a particular type of aircraft exceeded the allocated number of hours, the schedule was considered manageable. As the two figures approached each other, flight operations knew that things got tight. Once allocated pay hours exceeded the maximum capability, aircraft and/or flights had to be rescheduled to bring the two into balance. One commonly used technique was to try to substitute one type of aircraft where excess pilot hours existed on a flight series for another type of aircraft where pilot hours were scarce. For example, it might be possible to substitute a B-757 for a B-767 run providing that the B-757 was not already committed or that an alternate adjustment could be made.

After reviewing these figures for the past four weeks, flight operations became increasingly concerned. Compiled only five days earlier, the last Flight Operations Manpower Planning Report for December indicated a shortage in pilot hours of 485 hours for the B-727 and of 360 hours for the B-737 (see Exhibit 7-2). Even if the aggregate number of pilot hours equaled the hours required, there could be schedule problems. Flight operations felt that it was necessary to have a few extra hours (perhaps 1 or 2 percent) to accommodate mislocations of pilots or other problems that tended to arise once specific schedules had to be filled.

The figures shown in Exhibit 7-2 assumed "poor" December weather conditions. While the company felt reasonably confident in the forecasts as stated in the Flight Operations Manpower Planning Report, the individuals responsible for scheduling were concerned by recent long-term weather forecasts. If there were good weather, the demand for pilot hours would be substantially lower and CT would just meet the required hours.

General flying conditions over the northern tier of the country had been the worst in years during November and had caused considerable delays as well as stranded crews at all major airports. Constitutional's meteorologists were forecasting continued fog along the Middle Atlantic states and considerable sleet and icing around the northeastern airports. These monthly forecasts had been accurate approximately 70 percent of the time and were taken into account in CT's manpower planning reports. In other words, CT felt that there was a 70 percent probability that the manpower requirements summarized in Exhibit 7-2 would be what they would experience, while there was approximately a 30 percent probability that there would be weather that would allow the company enough pilot hours to avoid schedule failure.

The use of supervisors as pilots in a pinch in December would do little more than accommodate flight operations' desire for a 1 to 2 percent margin of safety in good weather.

COMPETITION

Flight operations was concerned as to what effect the actions of CT's competitors would have on this situation. Trans Continental, another large carrier and CT's chief rival along the northern tier, did not normally add as many flights to the winter schedule as Constitutional. This was because Trans Continental's route system was more diversified than CT's and subject to less seasonality regarding the overall demand on the system.

However, North American Airlines, which was experiencing relatively poor pilot relations, had announced that pilot hours for the month were already known to be particularly tight. Nevertheless, North American was not expected to cancel any flights during the early part of December and would probably try to operate its entire schedule as published.

EXHIBIT 7-2 Flight Operations Manpower Planning Report, December 1988

	Crew Pay Hours		
	Maximum Capability (available)	Allocated (required)	Margin Above or Below Allocated Pay Hours
B-727	43,295	43,780	− 485
B-737	29,795	30,155	− 360
B-747	3,825	3,675	+ 150
B-757	3,500	3,555	− 55
B-767	2,630	2,565	+ 65

QUESTIONS

1. Why does Constitutional Airlines find itself short of pilots in such a critical period as the month of December? Do you think it was a wise decision by management not to carry extra pilots on the payroll to cover the peak in December? (Assume that a B-727 cockpit crew costs $180,000 per year, for example, 3 pilots times $60,000 per crew member per year.) Determine the following:

a. Estimated revenue:
block-to-block hrs/crew (.80 × crew hrs/mo)
× average B-727 block-to-block speed
× average B-727 number of seats
× 12 cents/mi. (est. revenue/seat mile)
× load factor (est. December load factor) = estimated revenue

b. Estimated direct operating expenses:
(flight operations, maintenance & psgr. svs.):
est. rev. × 60% (est.) = estimated direct operating expenses

c. Contribution to overhead and profits:
estimated revenue – estimated direct operating expenses

2. What are the potential economic impacts of cancellation in early December compared to a strategy of doing nothing? Develop a decision tree including the following possibilities: (a) cancel early—no substitution of crew hours; (b) cancel early—substitution of crew hours; (c) do nothing, forced to cancel late—no substitution of crew hours; (d) do nothing, forced to cancel late—substitution of crew hours; (e) do nothing, good weather allows no cancellations. (Assume a load factor of 60 percent for early December, 1–15 and 68 percent for late December, 16–31.) Remember that revenue is associated with block-to-block hours, which equals crew hours × .80.

3. Which alternative would you recommend? Why?

Introduction
Marketing Game Plan
Measuring the Results

8
GLOBAL AIRLINES Marketing

INTRODUCTION

Global Airlines (GL) launched a comprehensive marketing program in Metropolitan City. This effort, the first of such magnitude for GL in a major city, had two objectives: (1) to increase market share and (2) to determine if an intensive marketing program could have an effect on the carrier's image and its sales and boardings. Metropolitan City was selected as the test market because it represented a major area with a typical mix of business and vacation travel. Moreover, in Metropolitan City, GL was very competitive with other carriers over medium and long-haul segments. In addition, because Metropolitan City had a single major newspaper and relatively few radio and TV stations, it was considered to be a good area in which to conduct the intensive marketing program test. Three million people lived in the Metropolitan City market.

Global's major long-haul competition in the Metropolitan City market came from Allied Air Lines and Great Northern Airlines. Other regional carriers competed for shorter travel business throughout the area. Exhibit 8-1 indicates the major nonstop destinations of the three major lines serving Metropolitan City. Prices stabilized in recent years after the turbulent decade following deregulation. Nonprice competition once again prevailed with each carrier trying to distinguish its service through the quality of its flight schedule—frequency of departures and connecting service—baggage service, and in-flight service. Allied Air Lines enjoyed a competitive advantage through its service to more cities throughout the United States. Global had the advantage of service to Europe and the Far East. A frequently used measure of competitive success in the Metropolitan City area was the share of the passenger market on nonstop flights to leading destinations such as New York, Chicago, Washington, D.C., and Los Angeles. On this basis, market shares were as follows for two important segments:

	Market Share (%)		
Flight Segment	*Great Northern*	*Global*	*Allied*
Metropolitan City–New York	32	36	32
Metropolitan City–Chicago	35	24	41

Global's intensive marketing program test was an integrated marketing effort using personal sales, advertising, sales promotion, and publicity. Like its competitors, Global invested heavily in national and local advertising. Its total advertising budget of approximately 3 percent of sales amounted to $18 million. In the company's total communication effort, advertising sought to reach both consumer and industrial mar-

EXHIBIT 8-1 Major Nonstop Destinations from Metropolitan City for Great Northern, Global, and Allied

	Number of Daily Scheduled Flights by Airline		
Destination	*Great Northern*	*Global*	*Allied*
Boston	—	1	—
Chicago	7	6	10
Denver	—	2	5
Detroit	1	1	1
Kansas City	—	1	—
Las Vegas	—	1	—
Los Angeles	—	13	26
New York	5	5	6
Phoenix	1	1	—
St. Louis	—	1	—
Washington, D.C.	—	2	22

kets. The advertising budget was divided as follows for major media:

Media	*Percentage*
Newspapers	39%
Radio	31
Television	13
Magazines	15
Outdoor and public transportation	2
Total	100%

Most of the advertising done by Global was local in nature, featuring destinations and departure times. The company's 300-person passenger sales force called on a variety of present and potential customers, including travel agents; corporate traffic managers; federal, state, and local government officials; military installations; and key executives in smaller businesses that did not have sufficient travel demands to warrant a traffic department. A special cargo sales force sold Global's air freight services. The Global passenger sales representative typically was assigned a territory with all types of accounts. As a rule, the sales representative made very few cold calls. Rather, the selling effort took the form of assisting in special travel problems such as consulting on charter flights, designing procedures for improving the processing of reservations and billings, handling complaints, and explaining new service features. Frequently, a representative was called on to assist in getting a reservation for a key executive or government official. Often, the salesperson knew not only the traffic manager but also the principals in the organization and through repeated service was able to build up a close working relationship between the customer and Global.

In individual businesses it was often difficult to determine who made the decision to fly with a particular carrier. Typically, an executive had a schedule to meet that permitted some leeway in departure time and passed on the request for airline space to a secretary or to the company traffic department. A secretary might make the selection, often on the basis of personal preference or advice from a travel agent. At times, however, an executive would specify preference for a particular carrier, particularly if he or she was a member of a frequent flier program with the carrier. If recent experience had been unfavorable, there might be a standing request to avoid a particular carrier. Travel agents were also influential in airline selection, indicating preferences, when possible, to those airlines that in their judgment had the best service record. Many of the larger travel agents served as the sole representative of selected businesses in their respective markets.

Global made annual surveys of its service, including reservation procedures. From these surveys it was apparent that the methods used to place a reservation were divided as follows:

Who Made Reservation	*Percentage (%)*
Passenger direct	16
Travel agent	51
Corporate traffic department*	10
Secretary*	15
Other*	8

*Direct or through travel agent.

MARKETING GAME PLAN

Against this background of airline promotion and consumer buying patterns Global's Metropolitan City intensive marketing program was developed. The total program, including personal selling, sales promotion, advertising and publicity was budgeted at $470,000, broken down as follows:

Advertising	$290,000
Hospitality flights	50,000

Sales representatives	45,000
Local promotions	65,000
Film festival contribution	20,000

Advertising expenditures shown in the Metropolitan City market area represented an increase over normal of approximately 125 percent for a six-week period. Funds for the intensive marketing program would come from the currently budgeted advertising and promotional program, diverted from other markets.

As indicated in Exhibit 8-2, the media plan for the intensive marketing plan did not deviate significantly from Global's originally scheduled media allocation pattern. With the introduction of the intensive marketing program, however, new advertisements were created for TV, radio, and newspaper. These ads stressed the point that Metropolitan City was a wonderful place in which to live and work—but those who had to leave the city would find flying with Global a real pleasure.

To augment the Metropolitan City sales force of 26, three teams of 25 sales representatives were brought in from Global's worldwide system, each team for a one-week period. This supplementary personal selling effort was directed at prospective passenger and cargo accounts and travel agents. From a list of 12,000 business firms with 10 or more employees, all current key Global accounts (those accounts buying more than $10,000 annually from Global) were eliminated. In addition, certain classes of businesses, theaters, service stations, laundries, and restaurants that had minimal travel needs were allocated among the three sales teams with each person assigned a specific territory. Within each of the 25-person teams, 20 were assigned to call on the prospective customers generated from this list, and five were detailed to call on a special list of potential air cargo accounts. The 20 sales representatives contacting the firms listed on the prospect list were expected to complete 20 calls daily if their list was in downtown Metropolitan City, 15 calls for other segments of the area. In their sales presentation they would feature the Global airline credit card, the Write Your Own Ticket program whereby the customer could write his or her own ticket once there was confirmation that space was available, and the special advantages enjoyed by Global because of its system coverage worldwide as well as in the United States. In the process of making their calls, the sales representatives were expected to determine the air travel needs of the business. Their estimate of the potential air travel, including destinations, could then be passed on to the regular Metropolitan City sales force. Global also planned to send a personal letter as a follow-up to all of these potential accounts, and as many as possible would be called on by the Metropolitan City sales force in subsequent months.

Coupled with Global's advertising and personal selling in the intensive marketing program were a variety of publicity and public relations

EXHIBIT 8-2 Metropolitan City Intensive Media Program Compared to Regular Media Program

	Original Schedule		Total Expanded Program	
Area Newspapers	*No. of Ads*	*Size (average)*	*No. of Ads*	*Size (average)*
12	37	6,900 lines	49	14,380 lines
Radio	*Spots per Week*		*Spots per Week*	
AM spots	131		186	
FM spots	8		105	
Television	*Spots per Week*		*Spots per Week*	
60-second spots	7		10	
20-second sports	8		20	
Outdoor	*Number*		*Number*	
Signs	141		383	
Bus posters	50		280	

efforts. Ten 30-minute scenic flights in Boeing 767 jets were scheduled over the area. These flights were to be heavily advertised on radio and in newspapers. A charge of $10 per person would be made for these flights. In addition, during the same period, two Royal Service meal flights of two hours each were scheduled. Each of these flights would accommodate 100 guests plus Global representatives. Guests for these flights would include members of the local chambers of commerce and Junior League, key traffic management representatives, travel agents, business leaders, civic officials, and the press. Special attention on one of these flights would be given to members of Metropolitan City's Film Festival Committee, a group of socially prominent people who sponsored the festival each year. Because the film festival was a major civic affair, a black-tie dinner was scheduled at one of Metropolitan City's leading hotels at which Global would make a contribution to the Film Festival Committee of approximately $20,000. About 400–500 guests were expected to attend the dinner, hosted by Global's top officials.

In the area of sales promotion, window displays were to be placed in 200 travel agent offices for one month. Windows and in-store displays were also to be featured over the six-week period in a number of Metropolitan City's leading department stores. Two round-trip tickets to Vienna were to be auctioned off on a local television station. Five separate direct mailing advertising efforts were scheduled weekly. Each of these mailings to 15,000 names carried a special message. For example, one mailing was a European tour folder with a reply card offering a full selection of seven other specially designed European tour folders. Another special effort called for luncheon meetings with top officials of key companies in the area. These luncheons featured the Royal Service menu and brief talks by Global executives.

A bonus of 3,500 miles was given to individuals signing up for Global's frequent flier program during the six-week period. Special rates were developed in cooperation with two rental car companies and several area hotels for individuals flying into Metropolitan City on Global during the intensive marketing program.

MEASURING THE RESULTS

In planning the intensive marketing program test in Metropolitan City, the Global executives recognized that they had no previous measurement guidelines for promotions of this scope. They felt that no accurate dollar forecast of incremental revenue could be made and that no specific quota could be set for the Metropolitan City sales office. However, they planned to analyze the forecasted sales and boardings in the Metropolitan City area to determine the beneficial effects of the program. In addition, certain specific efforts were launched to measure the effect of the program on Global's image.

A nationally known political polling firm was engaged to measure before, during, and after consumer awareness and attitudes toward the three airlines in the area. The firm outlined the direction their research would take in a letter to Global's director of marketing research.

First, before launching the intensive marketing program, they would determine the entire spectrum of attitudes toward Global among air travelers and nontravelers in the area. Then, approximately six weeks later, they would check again to determine what impression, if any, was made by the six-week promotion and marketing campaign. Finally, about six months later, they would make a final survey to determine the Global image, again looking for change.

The company planned to interview 1,100 air travelers, defining them as people who made one or more flights during the past year. To find these travelers and interview them in depth would involve contacting a minimum of 3,240 adult travelers. A different sample population would be interviewed in each of the following phases.

Phase I

This interviewing phase would be done over a 10-day period just before the launch. It would involve 300 air travelers, selected at random from a sample that encompassed the entire area and that was stratified by income to achieve economical interviewing: 100 travelers who earn more than $50,000 per year, 100 who earn between $25,000 and $50,000, and 100 who earn less than $25,000. In addition, 100 neighbors who are not air travelers or only occasional air travelers would be interviewed. These, too, would be distributed evenly among the three income groups.

Phase II

This interviewing would be done during a two-week period almost immediately after the promotion campaign. Again, 300 air travelers would be interviewed. Of these, 100, the same people interviewed in Phase I, would be the panel, the other 200 would be new air travelers, a matched sample but not a panel. In addition, 100 neighbors who have not traveled by air in the past year would be interviewed.

Phase III

This interviewing would be done approximately six months after termination of the campaign. Again, 300 air travelers would be interviewed, including 100 from Phase II. However, there are dangers in interviewing the same people on three occasions. Thus, of the 200 new air travelers interviewed in Phase II, 100 would be reinterviewed in Phase III. Two hundred new air travelers and 100 neighbors who have not traveled during the past year would also be interviewed.

The firm planned to gather five kinds of information:

1. *Travel habits.* Number of flights, distance, class, reservation methods, airline preference.
2. *Airline image and visibility.* Limited to the major transcontinental carriers out of Metropolitan City, Great Northern, Allied, and Global, to find out which airlines are preferred and why.
3. *Traveler profiles.* The types who prefer each of the three major airlines would be analyzed. In other words, the researchers would describe those who prefer Global in terms of sex, income, occupation, age, religion, ethnic background, state of origin, type of business, area of residence, and, most important, in terms of their reading habits and the other ways that they absorb information. The same would be done for Great Northern and Allied because a comparison would add measurably to an understanding of each airline's image.
4. *Airline service performance.* An essential element in total airline image is to get a performance rating on each phase of ground and in-flight service. This includes reservations, ticketing, airport facilities, check-in, class configuration, flight attendants, ground personnel, meals, beverage service, in-flight motion pictures, keeping passengers informed, equipment, baggage handling, and other such items.

5. *Cargo users.* The researchers would determine how many in the sample have ever used airline cargo service. They would get an evaluation of each carrier's cargo services and a report on each shipper's experience with each airline. Then cargo experiences would be related to attitudes and preferences for passenger travel.

In conducting its surveys, the company interviewer would ask a number of questions that dealt with air travel and interviewee demographic characteristics, but the key questions would be related to the respondent's attitudes toward the three airlines. To measure these attitudes, a number of different questions were used. The following questions (not sequential, but scattered throughout the questionnaire) are illustrative.

- Let's say you're making a trip to the East Coast and Great Northern, Global, and Allied all have a flight that leaves about the same time for your destination. Which of the three airlines would you choose? You don't have to be familiar with them. Let's say you were suddenly faced with the choice. As of now, which would you prefer—Great Northern, Global, or Allied? Which one would be your second choice?

	First Choice	Second Choice
Great Northern	________	________
Global	________	________
Allied	________	________

- I'm going to read you some words and phrases. For each one, I want you to tell me if you think it applies *mainly* to Great Northern, *mainly* to Global, or *mainly* to Allied. Any one may apply to two or all three airlines, but I want you to tell me which *one* you think it applies to the *most*. If you haven't had experience on the airlines, just give your impression or feeling.

	Great Northern	Global	Allied	None or All Same
Civic minded	______	______	______	______
Conservative	______	______	______	______
Good investment	______	______	______	______
Luxurious	______	______	______	______
Flashy	______	______	______	______
Glamorous	______	______	______	______
Reliable	______	______	______	______
Big	______	______	______	______
Experienced	______	______	______	______
Careful	______	______	______	______

	Great Northern	Global	Allied	None or All Same
Polite	______	______	______	______
Efficient	______	______	______	______
Good service	______	______	______	______
Friendly	______	______	______	______
For businesspeople	______	______	______	______
Modern	______	______	______	______
Clean	______	______	______	______
For families	______	______	______	______

- Of the three airlines—Great Northern, Global, and Allied—which one do you feel has the most frequent service to New York from Metropolitan City? Which of the three has the fewest flights from here to New York?

	Most	Least
Great Northern	______	______
Global	______	______
Allied	______	______
All same	______	______

- Now I want to read you some statements. For each one I want to know if you tend to agree or disagree.

	Agree	Disagree	Indifferent
All three major airlines are good, but Allied provides just a little extra care.	______	______	______
Global used to have a flashy image, but now it is coming through as efficient and reliable.	______	______	______
Great Northern is most likely to go where you want to go, when you want to go.	______	______	______
All three major airlines are good on safety, but I give a little edge to Global.	______	______	______
Of the three, Global is most versatile. They handle cargo and fly overseas in addition to domestic passenger service.	______	______	______

Allied may not be so glamorous, but they make up for it with care and extra service.	________	________	________
Great Northern is likely to be a little impersonal.	________	________	________
Of the three, Global seems to be coming on the fastest.	________	________	________
Allied moves slowly in adopting new ideas.	________	________	________
Global is likely to be a little more luxurious and comfortable than the other two.	________	________	________

- Now I want you to rate the total performance of each airline, taking everything into consideration. Rate each of the carriers using 1 as the best possible score and 5 as very unsatisfactory.

	1	2	3	4	5
Great Northern	_____	_____	_____	_____	_____
Global	_____	_____	_____	_____	_____
Allied	_____	_____	_____	_____	_____

Global executives, in general, were enthusiastic about the proposed awareness and attitude measurement plan for the intensive marketing program. This was the first time that such an elaborate measurement program had been undertaken in a single market. Within the Global executive group, however, a word of caution was suggested by the company's vice president of advertising. Prior to the intensive marketing program, he had written to the director of marketing research as follows:

Undoubtedly, we will get some useful information from the forthcoming study. However, there is one area of concern that I have, and I pass it on to you for what it is worth. What troubles me is that the advertising, which is the most costly element in the program, is uniquely designed to create attitudinal shifts. Apparently, a shift in the area of five points may be necessary in order to achieve a statistically significant change in the sample being used. I am not at all sure that any blitz, and ours is certainly experimental, can deliver at such a level.

Most advertising has the obvious responsibility of registering specific messages, which is more easily measurable, and is actually something we have measured successfully in the past. When doing this, we have also probed for attitudinal changes, usually with a notable lack of success, and it is this experience that makes me flag a possible trouble spot. The intensive marketing program advertising is different in that it is clearly designed to change attitudes, and we may have to be content with relatively small shifts in attitudes that are built on years of flying experience in many cases..

In the final analysis, of course, the real test of the intensive marketing program would be in increased Global boardings out of Metropolitan City. Data that could be used to evaluate the program would indicate Global's own load factor as well as similar data for Great Northern and Allied Air Lines. No specific plans had been set for appraising the effectiveness of the personal selling element in the intensive marketing program. Some Global executives felt that, while this was a small part of the program's total budget, it could be the most significant element in the total program.

QUESTIONS

1. What is your evaluation of Global's intensive marketing program?

2. What problems do you foresee as Global attempts to evaluate the intensive marketing program?

3. How would you go about measuring the effectiveness of the program?

Background
Airline Economics
Mid-America's Decision

9
MID-AMERICA AIRLINES
Fleet Planning

BACKGROUND

Mid-America Airlines (MA) grew considerably since deregulation and in recent years enjoyed an above-average 13 percent return on investment (ROI). However, the company achieved this partially by an increased debt-to-equity ratio of 3:1. Despite their highly leveraged position, the company planned to purchase an average of 1,400 seats of aircraft capacity each year for the next six years, in response to a forecasted growth of 15 to 20 percent per year. There were some doubts about MA being able to raise the capital required in the financial market.

Management must decide whether the company should opt for wide-body aircraft at lower purchase prices per seat of available capacity, low cost of production per seat mile, and spacious appearance. The smaller, narrow-body aircraft appear to have lower break-even load factors, which permit more frequent departures and are economically attractive to operate on short trips because of the reduced take-off costs. Mid-America must determine what type of capacity is best suited for its operations and competitive strategy.

The questions being asked by management of its planning staff are:

1. Are wide-bodies inherently more economic than our present aircraft types?
2. Can they be deployed on our domestic route structure profitably?
3. How will they affect our competitive situation in terms of market share and frequency of service?

AIRLINE ECONOMICS

The airlines use "available seat mile" (ASM), one passenger seat flown one mile, rather than a "passenger mile" flown, as the unit of production because air carriers' *costs* are directly related to the number of *seats* rather than the number of *passengers* flown over a given distance. Once an airplane is scheduled on a particular flight, the total cost of that flight varies only slightly with the number of passengers that the plane is carrying.

It is an industry rule of thumb that the variable cost of adding an extra passenger to a flight amounts to only 10 percent of the fare paid by that passenger and that the remaining 90 percent contributes directly to operating profit. The cost per unit of production is influenced by a variety of factors, including aircraft type and average length of flights. Given this cost per available seat mile, an airline's total operating costs are approximated by multiplying total ASMs by cost per ASM and adding to this "fixed" or ASM-related cost the "variable" cost of 10 percent passenger fares.

Airline costs are, perhaps, less fixed than the industry rule indicates, except in the very short run. Over time spans of a year or more, the industry's growth rate and inflation tends, in effect, to make other "fixed" ASM-related costs, such as depreciation and salaries, variable.

Although costs are tied most closely to available seat miles, the revenue generated on a flight is directly related to (1) the number of passengers carried, (2) how far they are flown, and (3) how much these passengers paid per mile of flight. The product of the first two factors is revenue passenger miles (RPMs). The third term is commonly called yield per RPM.

Given the high proportion of costs that are fixed, profits are very sensitive to the load factor experienced by an airline. In addition, because a large percentage of fixed costs are associated with take-off and landing operations, the average cost per ASM of longer flights is substantially lower.

There is also a close correlation between an airline's share of passengers flown over a route and the number of seats that the airline flew over the route. Characteristically, however, on a competitive route served by two or more carriers, the dominant carrier in terms of seats flown attracts slightly more than its proportionate share of passengers over that route.

Historically, there has been a marked tendency for competing airlines to fly similar aircraft over the same routes. This is because all carriers are facing similar economics and the analyses carried out by planners for different airlines leads them to select similar aircraft. One form of competition over these routes has been the addition of more frequent flights, increasing the share of seats flown and the share of passengers flown. This form of competition, with similar competitive responses, is thought to contribute materially to overcapacity situations on many routes, resulting in losses for some carriers.

Load Factors and the Equipment Cycle

Since profitability is so sensitive to the load factor, it would seem that the industry would be concerned with maintaining profitable load factor levels through a policy of restraint in adding capacity. However, with the great advances in technology and improved economic performance of aircraft in the three decades of the '60s, '70s, and '80s, the airlines undertook massive re-equipment programs. Pressure to keep up with other airlines resulted in the entire industry going through cycles of buying more capacity than the growth of the market justified. A prominent industry trend has been toward faster, larger, and more fuel-efficient aircraft such as the two-engine B-757 and B-767. Unfortunately, because of its capital-constrained position, MA was not able to consider any of these newer aircraft at this time. Consequently, it was looking at the used aircraft market where a number of older aircraft were becoming available at attractive prices. Each aircraft type has its own particular optimization in terms of cost per ASM over a specific range. Generally speaking, total cost per ASM includes fixed and variable elements and decreases on a per unit basis as distance increases.

MID-AMERICA'S DECISION

Mid-America was focusing on DC-10s and L-1011s because of their favorable economics over quite short routes. These wide-body tri-jets combined the maneuverability and ease of operation of the B-747 with the ability to fly in and out of small airports. The wide-body aircraft MA was considering compared to a smaller jet of the B-727 variety as follows:

Estimates	*B-727*	*Wide-body*
Investment (including spare (parts)	$8,500,000	$18,750,000
Seats (low density seating)	125	300
Effective maximum economic range	1,700	2,800

Arguments in Favor of Wide-Bodies

The planning department pointed out that the wide-bodies were not only likely to stimulate primary demand because of greater flying comfort, they also operated at lower cost per ASM (even on shorter routes) and, therefore, they had greater profit potential. Admittedly they used more fuel, but fuel consumed per ASM was actually slightly lower than that experienced with smaller aircraft. All in all, it was felt that the wide-body was technologically a better aircraft.

It was also pointed out that fewer aircraft would be needed to fill the ASM gap and fewer operations would facilitate scheduling. However, the planning department also felt that large aircraft would be less flexible to meet short-term fluctuations in specific city-pair markets.

Finally, it was mentioned that wide-body aircraft could best provide for MA's faster-than-industry growth. MA was experiencing growth in primary demand and market share in most of the markets it served. This would favor the operation of larger aircraft that were most profitable in high-density routes.

EXHIBIT 9-1 Return on Investment (ROI) as a Function of Passengers Carried and Stage Length (Figures in Percent)

	Wide-Body Tri-Jet—300 Seats— Number of Passengers/Flight				
Stage Length (miles)	*50*	*75*	*125*	*200*	*300*
500	−19.3	−10.4	7.4	34.1	69.7
1,000	−15.6	−3.7	20.0	55.6	103.0
1,500	−13.4	−0.2	26.6	66.5	119.9
2,000	−13.0	2.0	32.0	77.0	136.9

	Boeing 727—125 Seats— Number of Passengers/Flight				
Stage Length (miles)	*50*	*75*	*125*	*200**	*300**
500	−19.8	6.9	45.6	26.2	26.2
1,000	1.1	24.7	76.2	50.5	50.5
1,500	4.8	33.8	91.8	62.8	62.8
2,000	Maximum range 1700 miles				

* Multiple flights

EXHIBIT 9-2 Analysis of Markets: 66 Top MA City-Pair Markets

City-Pairs with MA 1988 Estimated Market Share < 50%

Stage Length Miles	*Average Number Passengers Carried by MA/Day 0–200*	*201–300*	*301–500*	*501–900*	*> 900*
< 750	7	4	1	0	0
750–1,249	3	0	2	0	0
1,250–1,750	1	0	1	0	0
> 1,750	0	0	0	0	0

City Pairs with MA 1988 Estimated Market Share > 50%

Stage Length Miles	*AverageNumber Passengers Carried by MA/Day 0–200*	*201–300*	*301–500*	*501–900*	*> 900*
< 750	14	17	4	1	1
750–1,249	2	2	2	0	0
1,250–1,750	0	1	1	1	0
> 1,750	0	0	1	0	0

Arguments Against Wide-Bodies

The marketing department was apprehensive about the use of wide-bodies on Mid-America's route structure at this time. They pointed out that, in terms of density and length of haul, MA could not economically apply a wide-body. It was noted that MA's most dense route was ranked 28th on the list of the most dense routes served by the domestic airline industry.

Marketing also indicated that people do not generally ask what aircraft they will be flying when they call reservations. Departure time is more important and an airline serves the consumer by proper scheduling. In conclusion, marketing favored the greater flexibility of scheduling the smaller-capacity B-727.

The Need for Data

Management felt that the Oil City-Oakton market would be appropriate for the introduction of wide-bodies. Demand over this 810-mile route amounted to approximately 650,000 passengers per year (one way) of which MA carried 257,400. It was expected that demand in this market would grow by about 15 to 20 percent per year over the next five years. On weekdays (260/yr), when the bulk of this demand occurred, MA served this route with 10 flights in each direction. On weekends (104/yr), MA offered 8 flights per day.

Management believed that it would be possible to finance the necessary investment in the used equipment now available. The planning staff developed an approximate return on investment (ROI) that might be expected for the B-727 and DC-10 or L-1011 for a variety of passenger levels and stage lengths (see Exhibit 9-1). Exhibit 9-2 summarizes the city-pair markets being served by MA in 1988.

QUESTIONS

1. Evaluate the relative costs of the DC-10/L-1011 type aircraft and the B-727 aircraft. How much difference in capital investment would Mid-America Airlines be required to make if it were to add DC-10/L-1011 type aircraft compared to B-727 aircraft over the next six years?

2. Prepare a recommendation for MA management.

Introduction
Objectives of the IA Pilots
Objectives of the Company
ALPA Events Leading to the Negotiations

10
INTERNATIONAL AIR CHARTER NEGOTIATIONS
Labor Relations

INTRODUCTION

The employment and working agreement between International Air Charter (IA) and their pilots, represented by the Air Line Pilots Association (ALPA), was amendable on July 1, 1988. Four months prior to the amendable date, the IA pilots' Master Executive Council (MEC) appointed a negotiating committee, consisting of five line pilots, for the purpose of developing amendments to the contract and negotiating a tentative agreement. The committee drew up a summary of proposals that included 40 items of revision (see Exhibit 10-1). The summary of proposals was submitted to the MEC in Chicago in May 1988. The MEC approved the amendments.

OBJECTIVES OF THE IA PILOTS

The negotiating committee was directed by the MEC to conclude a tentative agreement on all 40 issues as soon as possible. Reduction of monthly flight time limitations from 80 hours to 75 hours was the pivotal amendment. Additionally, the committee was instructed to explore tax-sheltered areas of benefits. It was the majority consensus of the MEC that the IA pilots were below the airline industry in wages and working conditions and some gains had to be made in these two areas. A cost-of-living wage increase was considered minimal, and the target contract life was to be 18 months. The severe financial posture of the company was recognized as a constraining factor.

Pressures Acting on the Pilots' Negotiating Committee

Rising Costs and Recessionary Pressures in the Airline Industry. In 1987 IA lost $47.9 million, and announced that it anticipated losing $70–80 million in 1988. For 1989 a company forecast indicated a loss of nearly $50 million. It would not be until the third quarter of 1990 that IA would have a positive cash flow.

The perils of a high-cost contract under such conditions were apparent. It could move the company toward bankruptcy, a drastic cutback in routes, or a merger.

The traditional ambience of collective bargaining seemed inappropriate. The offensive committee, the defensive company, the implicit threat of a strike, the bluffing and challenges from each side, could only be counterproductive in this negative cash-flow business environment.

One financial columnist predicted that IA would exhaust operating funds in mid-1989. Indeed, it was the opinion of the negotiating committee that there was a need for realistic appraisal and innovative techniques in the collective bargaining since the survival of the company was not a certainty.

However, one active segment of the pilot group disagreed with this evaluation and premise. They contended that the essential elements of IA's loss posture were the result of poor management.

Industry Standards

Parity in the industry is extremely complex and difficult to define. The situation is exacerbated by deregulation and the wave of new nonunion carriers that have appeared. One of the most misused and controversial measures of industry standards is comparing pilot contracts and developing an annual forecast of pilots' annual earnings. A more valid evaluation is to compare annual W-2 statements of comparable pilot groups. Additionally, annual earnings forecasts only consider dollars and ignore other benefits.

IA management often argued against using wages as a sole measure of comparing pilot groups. They pointed out that an annual pass on IA permitted a pilot (and family) to fly all over the world. With a domestic carrier, the annual pass was more restrictive. Also, International Air Charter pilots flew long trip patterns or could bid a series of short trips close together, which would give them 14–30 days off duty. This allowed IA pilots to live in Europe and the Far East, which offered some attractive living arrangements including tax benefits. Few airlines could provide this opportunity.

Hidden wage benefits vary between airlines. A typical IA 747 captain received the equivalent of $25,000 a year in hidden wage benefits. Medical benefits, long-term disability, life insurance, voluntary personal accident plan, cooperative retirement income plan, cooperative income trust plan, social security, stock purchase plan, travel plan, vacations and holidays added up to an estimated $31,000 with the typical captain contributing only about $6,000 toward these benefits.

Flight working conditions on IA were somewhat easier than on other airlines because of its generally long flight segments. Only a few schedules contained the onerous short flight patterns of most domestic airlines.

Finally, parity must show some cognizance of the company's ability to pay. International Air Charter was going through a financially difficult period and prospects were not good for the immediate future. Profitability in the industry varies considerably between carriers. Unlike the prederegulation days when most carriers performed financially in accordance with the state of the national economy, today we find some carriers reporting record earnings while others are on the verge of bankruptcy. Nevertheless, the most recent contractual agreement in the industry generally becomes the industry standard and a target for subsequent negotiations.

Effective Date of Signing the Contract. Historically, IA pilot negotiations required 12–18 months to resolution. Because of the deferred date of signing and the extended median date of the life of the contract, IA pilots often presented opening demands at a higher level to compensate for the elongated negotiations. The length of bargaining could be controlled by the company using the various devices of the Railway Labor Act to continue work under the former contract; however, protracted collective bargaining was undesirable for pilots, since work rule benefits were not retroactive and wage increases usually only partly retroactive. The package that the pilots presented in the opening letter was estimated at 33 1/3 percent of the then current annual $73 million payroll. It is understandable that partial retroactivity and no work rule benefits, along with an increased cost profile of $2 million a month, were serious considerations.

The cost of negotiations could be substantial to ALPA. The five negotiators cost the association $30,000 a month. Expenses were about $10,000 each month. Office help and miscellaneous costs totaled about $5,000 per month. The MEC chairman and vice chairman participated in most of the negotiations at a flight pay loss rate of $7,000 per month. ALPA provided a professional negotiator as well as other experts at $6,500 per month. Other random costs brought the total monthly ALPA negotiations cost to about $60,000.

The difference between signing a contract at the amendable date of July 1, 1988, or one year later could be as much as $24 million in pay and benefits lost as well as a negotiating expense burden of $720,000. There would also be a dues loss to ALPA.

Morale would deteriorate with lengthy contract discussions and as months passed the erosion of morale would become pronounced and could have a serious effect on the pilot group.

Protracted collective bargaining had the downside risk of ending up in a slowdown or a work stoppage, which would cast a critical financial burden on the pilots, the association, and the company.

Public attitude also had a measurable influence on pilots. Little sympathy would be given for pilots in the inordinately high income bracket of flight crew members. As a result, on long negotiations, media were more likely to print company releases rather than those of the association. The result could be a public attitude of disdain, harassment, and apathy.

Specific Interests of Pilot Groups. Age and category were generally interrelated within pilot groups. Captains fell into the 45–60 age bracket with retirement mandatory at 60 years of age. Captains were biased toward better working conditions, improved retirement benefits, and tax-shelter advantages, and tended to be more complacent in their demands.

First officers ranged from 35 to 45 years of age. Their specific interest was in checking out as captain in order to obtain a wage increase. They were paid approximately 65 percent of the captain's pay and although they had a strong interest in increasing this percentage, they were also agreeable to increasing the pay of captains. They also sought stability in living and working conditions. Tax shelter benefits were important as well.

Second officers were the young pilots, 35 years of age and younger. They were the new hires and their jobs and domiciles were in continual flux. Security was a crucial consideration. Working conditions were, in great part, at the discretion of the company until the pilots acquired enough seniority to be assured they would not be furloughed. If second officers were upgraded, it was usually to Chicago as the first step. Should they elect another base, it was likely to be less stable than Chicago. Until second officers accrued substantial seniority, they had to program their lives in and out of the Chicago base until being upgraded. Second officers would typically be transient pilots until there was a substantial buffer, more than 20 percent, below them on the seniority list. When they moved from the second officer category to first officer, they moved to the bottom of that list and were subject to being moved again. They would also be subject to the blank line category. This category was the least desirable of pilot bidding for it placed pilots on call during the month, with little relief. They could be scheduled out on a trip around the world in a matter of hours.

Second officers' interests were in identification, pay, security, short-term benefits, base scheduling policies, and upgrading. They were more mobile, active, and sensitive to change in the pilot seniority system.

Cost of Living. The accepted annual rate of inflation was about 6 percent. Many pilots argued that all their costs increased 6 percent on an annual basis and a yearly raise of at least 6 percent was justified.

Tax Shelters. The membership and the MEC indicated a strong interest in tax-shelter devices.

Other Forms of Nonpay Remuneration. The pilot group considered increased travel benefits, increased optional insurance, improved medical plans, additional stock purchase plans, and other items as attainable and necessary to compensate for a lower pay demand.

Improved Work Rules. The committee was to examine both desired changes in work rules and also no-cost easement of work rules such as improved bid rights, new standby coverage, and an easement of certain onerous schedule patterns.

Recently Signed Contracts within the Company. The Transport Workers Union (TWU) had concluded a new working agreement which, they reported, made the maintenance service workers comparable with similar carriers in the industry. The members of that union received a 22 percent pay increase and a 20 percent supplemental benefit contract for a 36-month period. The payroll of the TWU was estimated at $83 million; that of the pilots, $73 million. Many pilots stated that ALPA should make gains equivalent to those of TWU. The company's response was that the TWU mechanics had been 10 percent behind the industry.

OBJECTIVES OF THE COMPANY

The board of directors of IA were aligned into two factions. One wanted to achieve profitability by reducing schedules and making a continuing effort to expand profitable routes. The other, which was willing to accept the short-term loss burden and to continue to fly all routes with certain exceptions, wanted to increase the airline routes and to move ahead to profitability as a longer-range goal.

It was in the best interests of the pilots to keep the airline in a growth pattern and stimulate route development.

Management wanted to expand the airline to meet the challenges of the 1990s and the growth in charter business. To do this they had to negotiate and obtain a reasonable and equitable contract with the pilots in a short length of time. Only then could they motivate the group to increase productivity and develop a sales program to increase traffic and sales.

If the negotiations followed the traditional lengthy course, it was likely that the movement forward to profitability would be endangered and a retrenchment program initiated.

Pressures on the Company

The following represent pressures acting on the company during the negotiations:

1. The increase in direct operating costs, due to such things as pilots' slowdowns.
2. The effect of profitability.
3. The morale of the pilots.
4. The effect of certain contractual obligations in future negotiations with other company unions—hospitalization, travel benefits, insurance, vacations, certain work rules, and other random variables.

5. Its responsibility to the stockholders.
6. The company negotiators' responsibility to management.
7. The affect of a contract on the long-range objectives of the company.
8. The effect of a strike.
9. The cost of negotiations in personnel and effort.
10. Maintaining flight schedules and integrity.

ALPA EVENTS LEADING TO THE NEGOTIATIONS

November 1987

Considering the conditions that then existed and those anticipated, a questionnaire was prepared and distributed to the pilots. The responses to this questionnaire were to be used in preparing a proposal for negotiating.

January 1988

On January 19, 1988, an MEC meeting was held in Chicago. This meeting was addressed by the chairman of the board of International Air Charter, who predicted that losses for IA in 1988 "could reach $70 million." At the meeting, the MEC chairman was elected and the negotiating committee was selected.

March 1988

A meeting of the MEC and the negotiating committee was held in Washington, D.C., to draft an opening letter to the company in light of the pilots' response to the questionnaire.

May 1988

A meeting of the MEC and the negotiating committee was held in Chicago to put the opening letter in its final form for presentation to the company. On May 27, 1988, the negotiating committee met for a session that lasted for five days. At this session they assembled 40 issues from the 111 questions voted on by the membership and other information sources. These 40 issues were approved by the MEC on June 2, 1988, in a three-day meeting in Chicago.

EXHIBIT 10-1 Summary of Proposals of the IA Pilots as Represented by the Air Line Pilots Association (ALPA)

1. Reduce monthly flight time limitations to seventy-five (75) credited hours per month, effective January 1, 1989.

   Monthly Maximum
   75 hours (from 80)

   BLH Minimum[1]
   66 hours (from 70)

   Monthly Minimum
   62 hours (from 65)

   It is proposed that when the airline goes on a 75-hour monthly limit:

   The Master Executive Council in coordination with the company may designate, for any base station by November 1st for the following year, two months (such as July and August) for which the monthly limit may be increased by five (5) hours (to eighty [80]) with the minima and guarantees remaining unchanged.

   The maximum pay hours shall remain at seventy-five (75) and the excess credited shall be banked.

2. Establish new rates of pay effective July 1, 1989, and provide an interim increase effective July 1, 1988. Rough calculations of this proposal produced the following sampling of yields based on 1/2 day, 1/2 night operation.

RATE OF PAY SCHEDULE
Effective July 1, 1989

	Per Hour (1/2–1/2)[2]	75 Hrs/ Month	66 Hrs/ Month	62 Hrs/ Month
B-747				
Captain—10th year	$140	$10,500	$9,240	$8,680
First officer—10th year	90	6,750	5,940	5,580
Second officer—6th year	50	3,750	3,300	3,100

[1]BLM minimum: blank line holder (BLH) is a pilot who does not have a definite flight schedule for the month. His or her pay guarantee is to be based on 66 hours. He or she is available for flights on short notice for the month with three 72 hours free of duty.

	Per Hour (1/2–1/2)[2]	75 Hrs/ Month	66 Hrs/ Month	62 Hrs/ Month
DC-10-30				
Captain—10th year	120	9,000	7,920	7,440
First officer—10th year	80	6,000	5,280	4,960
First officer—5th year	70	5,250	4,620	4,340
Second officer—5th year	50	3,750	3,300	3,100
B-727				
Captain—10th year	90	6,750	5,940	5,580
First officer—10th year	60	4,500	3,960	3,720
First officer—5th year	50	3,750	3,300	3,100

a. Effective July 1, 1988, through December 31, 1988, the total hourly pay to be paid to pilots at the increased hourly rate shall be multiplied by a factor of .8873 (to produce an increase of 6 percent over present pay for captains and first officers).

b. Effective January 1, 1989, through June 30, 1989, the total hourly pay to be paid to pilots at the increased rate shall be multiplied by a factor of .9465 (to produce the same monthly yield for 75 credited hours in January 1989 as for 80 credited hours in December 1988).

3. Provide that a pilot transferred to any operating crew position will be given full longevity credit for pay purposes.

4. Seniority as a pilot with the company shall begin with the pilot's date of employment as set forth on the pilot's system seniority list and shall continue to accrue during the period of service and furlough.[3]

5. A furloughed pilot shall be reinstated to active service within ten (10) years or a period of time equal to his or her accrued length of service as a pilot prior to being furloughed, whichever is greater, with no loss of seniority.

6. A pilot who is a transition training pilot for a portion of a month shall receive 2.33/2.20 credited hours for each day assigned as a transition training pilot. Such credit shall be applicable to the monthly limit. The present rate for pilots assigned as transition

[2]1/2 day hours, 1/2 night hours.

[3]Pilots presently lose seniority while on furlough. This amendment provides for the pilot to keep his or her original date of hire for the term of employment as a pilot. Other airlines permit pilots to keep original dates of hire. If IA pilots did not make this alteration, a merger using date of hire might adversely affect many pilots.

training pilots is 2.20 credited hours. The rate will be 2.33 when the flight time limitation is reduced to 75 hours/month.

7. Provide that a pilot deadheading, transferring, traveling to or from temporary assignment, to or from a training location, or on any other company business shall:

a. If traveling on company aircraft, travel in the first class section. The pilot may be displaced only by 100 percent full fare paying passengers, and by the following company personnel and their spouses: chairman and directors of the board, president, executive vice president, senior vice president, vice presidents, assistant vice presidents, treasurer, and comptroller.

b. If traveling on another carrier, travel in the first class section if such accommodation is available.

8. Provide for blank line holder rotation. When the requirements for blank line holders are not met by bidding, then pilots shall be assigned in reverse order of seniority.

9. Provide that, within one (1) hour after the completion of training flights or line check flights, the pilot being checked or trained shall be provided with a signed original of the appropriate report form.

10. Provide that a pilot may elect to change the training captain assigned to his or her training.

11. Increase the hourly meal allowance of all layover stations to reflect actual cost increases.

12. Increase the hourly laundry, tip, and miscellaneous expense to reflect actual cost increases.

13. Provide that a pilot with thirty (30) days or more of accrued vacation shall be able to split his or her vacation into primary and secondary periods.

14. Provide that a pilot shall have no less than a sixty (60) day advance notice of any vacation award or assignment. Provide that in no event shall a pilot's vacation be changed or deferred during the last thirty (30) days of this sixty (60) day notice period without his or her consent.

15. Increase maximum accrual of sick pay credit from 400 hours to 500 hours. A pilot, as of the first day of any month requiring any sick pay credit withdrawal, will reaccrue such credit at the rate of six (6) hours per month to the highest accumulated total.

16. Provide that sick leave withdrawals for sickness or injuries for which workmen's compensation benefits are paid shall be reduced

in an amount proportionate to the workmen's compensation benefit.

17. A pilot who fails to meet the physical standards as established by the Federal Aviation Administration (including its waiver policy) in a company physical examination or a pilot who contends that he or she is not currently physically qualified for flight assignment may at his or her option have a review of his or her case.

18. Provide that pilots at their option may but shall not be required to take a company physical examination. The company may require a physical examination if a pilot is on leave of absence for a period longer than (1) year.

19. Provide for increased moving expense allowance for company-paid pilot transfers.

20. Provide for voluntary early retirement after twenty (20) years of service without company approval.

21. Increase company "A" fund[4] contributions from five percent (5%) of pilot's pay to eight percent (8%) of pilot's pay effective January 1, 1990.

22. Increase minimum normal retirement benefit from the "A" fund to \$1,600 per month. This minimum to be reduced by \$4 per month for each month of early retirement to a minimum of \$1,120 per month at age fifty (50) for retirement benefit and actuarily reduced from \$1,120 per month at age fifty (50). If a pilot retires with less than twenty (20) years of service as a pilot, the minimum retirement benefit computed above shall be reduced by five percent (5%) per year prorated monthly for each year of service less than twenty (20) years.

    A pilot retiring at age 60—\$1,600 per month; at age 50—\$1,120 per month; a pilot less than age 50 with 10 years seniority (5% × 10 years)—\$560 per month.

23. Provide that disability retirement minima computed on January 1, 1988 shall be \$2,400 per month from age fifty (50) to age sixty (60) reduced by three percent (3%) per year for retirement prior to age fifty (50).

24. Provide that interest payable for "A" fund withdrawals shall be computed at five percent (5%) compounded annually.

---

[4]Company "A" fund contribution is invested in interest-bearing securities such as treasury bills and bonds.

25. Increase company "B" fund[5] contributions from eight percent (8%) of pilot's pay to eleven percent (11%) of pilot's pay, effective January 1, 1989.
26. Provide pilots with increased group insurance benefits and alternative HMO plans.
27. Amend System Board of Adjustment agreement to speed up the determination of grievances as follows:
    a. To provide mandatory System Board member meetings during the first week of February, May, August, and November of each year.
    b. Grievances submitted by the MEC chairman shall be heard in the first instance by the five-person board.
    c. A grievance arising out of the dismissal of a pilot shall be heard in the first instance by the five-person board except that at the request of the grievant, it shall be heard in the first instance by a four-person board.
28. Revise the company's free and reduced transportation policy so as to permit:
    a. Use of employee identification card for the purchase of eighty percent (80%) discount travel in the first class section of IA aircraft. This privilege to be granted solely to employees of IA with five (5) years of service or more, their spouses, and eligible dependents over twelve (12) years of age.
    b. Reduced rate travel privileges for furloughed pilots for a period of ninety (90) days after initial date of furlough.
    c. Pilots at their expense to obtain from the company a color-photo identification card for their spouses designed to facilitate and control dependent ticket purchase and travel.
    d. Extend cockpit pass and reduced rate travel privileges to pilots who are on unpaid medical leave of absence.
    e. Provide more definitive language regarding ticketing and travel in the cockpit of company aircraft.
29. Establish procedures that foster training-to-proficiency for transition training pilots and ensure standardized and equitable treatment for those pilots that may experience marked difficulty during such a curriculum.

---

[5]Company "B" fund contribution is invested in common stocks. Most airlines are currently paying 11% of pilots' pay into this fund.

30. Allow any pilot who has been awarded a vacancy at a base station and who has not transferred to such base station or has not entered the flight portion of any training required by such an award, to file a preference for any vacancy or proffer in the system filed subsequent to such pilot's award. If any subsequent vacancy or proffer is for the same equipment as the original award and the pilot has not transferred, such pilot shall not be restricted from filing preferences.

31. A pilot called to jury duty shall receive the minimum monthly guarantee while on jury duty. In addition, such a pilot shall be considered a time-available pilot during the month.

32. To provide for a Letter of Understanding that provides no IA pilot shall report for duty or work as a pilot while in any way under the influence of alcohol, marijuana, cocaine, or hallucinatory drugs. A 24-hour rule does not guarantee this performance; therefore, it shall be dropped. The company and the IA pilots will not condone violation of this policy.

33. Provide unemployment compensation for overseas-based pilots.

34. Revise Memorandum of Agreement regarding Frankfurt Foreign Station allowance dated February 6, 1988, Paragraph 2, to read: "Effective July 1, 1988, the monthly housing element of the allowance shall be: captains—400 DM; first officers—600 DM.

    Captains receive other benefits and this disparity of monthly housing element of the allowance tends to equalize the imbalance.

35. Amend the term "flight time," which shall mean that period of time when an aircraft first moves or is moved from the ramp blocks for the purpose of flight, and ending when the aircraft is next secured at a ramp or unloading point. In the event a captain elects to delay starting engines, in accordance with the provisions of the above, and he or she options to have flight time begin at the time the aircraft would normally have departed, it shall apply for pay and credit purposes and monthly credited time.

36. Provide that a pilot who fills a temporary flying assignment shall be furnished transportation by air (if available) over the most direct route. If direct routing requires flights on other carriers, MEC approval must be received to pilots being scheduled on such flights.

37. Provide that MEC approval must be received prior to the scheduling of a pilot to deadhead on another carrier.

38. Allow a qualified and designated captain or first officer to serve as a member of a flight crew in a position other than that to which he or she is designated only if such pilot has given consent in writing.
39. Provide that the chairman of the Master Executive Council shall approve layover facilities and accommodations prior to the scheduling of pilots to utilize such facilities and accommodations.
40. The association maintains the right to introduce additional issues that may occur during the length of the negotiating period.

QUESTION

1. You have been hired by International Air Charter *or* the pilots to assist in the negotiations. Develop a negotiating strategy for either side based on the facts in the case and the airline environment of the early 1990s to justify your position. Clearly identify the major problems or key issues facing the side you have chosen. List the most important facts that relate to the problem or issue. After analyzing the situation, develop your negotiating strategy, including possible alternatives that might provide an amicable solution to the problem.

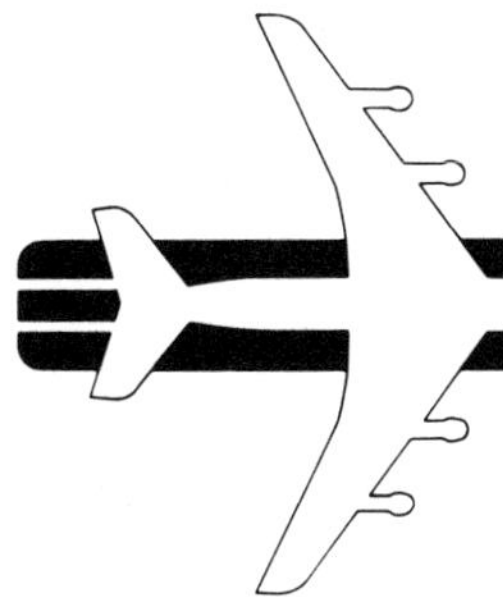

Background
Consultants' Summary View No. 1
Consultants' Summary View No. 2

11 WESTERN EXPRESS AIR LINES

Finances

BACKGROUND

Western Express (WE), a large regional carrier, was the result of a merger in April 1988 of West Aero Lines, Debon Air, and Pacific Coast Airlines, the names of which were changed as part of the merger to Western Express Air Lines.

West Aero Lines, incorporated in 1971 as a Washington corporation, inaugurated scheduled air service as a commuter in 1972. At the time of the merger West Aero was a regional carrier providing passenger, cargo, and mail service in the states of California, Idaho, Montana, Oregon, Utah, Washington, and in the province of Alberta.

Debon Air, incorporated in 1975 as a Nevada corporation, inaugurated scheduled service in 1976. At the time of the merger Debon Air provided passenger, cargo, and mail service primarily between Las Vegas-Reno, Reno-Phoenix, Phoenix-Los Angeles, Las Vegas-Los Angeles, and Las Vegas-San Diego.

Pacific Coast, incorporated in 1979 as a Delaware corporation, inaugurated scheduled service in 1980. At the time of the merger Pacific Coast was engaged primarily in scheduled commuter air service of passengers, cargo, and mail between various cities and towns within the state of California and from certain California cities and towns to Portland and Las Vegas. Pacific Coast was the only carrier that had a code-sharing agreement with a major carrier at the time of the merger. This agreement provided for joint ticketing, use of gate and ticket counter space, and interline baggage handling.

The route structure for the newly created Western Express is shown in Exhibit 11-1.

Employees

Western Express had approximately 3,890 employees in early 1989, of whom approximately 21 percent were nonunion administrative, supervisory, and clerical employees. The balance of the employees were covered by collective bargaining agreements with systemwide units. The contracts conformed generally to the pattern of labor agreements in the airline industry and expired on varying dates. Western Express considered its employee relations to be satisfactory.

Since the merger in 1988, WE had not been involved in any strike or work stoppage. In 1986, Pacific Coast sustained a strike during its negotiations with the International Association of Machinists. This lasted six days and terminated on the agreement on the terms of a three-year contract with that union. In 1987 employees of the Flight Attendants Union engaged in a "wildcat" strike during negotiations with that union which resulted in a two-day work stoppage. In July 1987, West Aero Lines experienced a strike by its passenger service employees that curtailed operations for one week.

EXHIBIT 11-1 Western Express Air Lines Route System

Domestic

1. Between the coterminal points San Francisco and Oakland, California, the intermediate points Sacramento, Santa Rosa, Marysville/Yuba City, Chico, Red Bluff/Redding, Eureka/Arcata, and Crescent City, California, and the terminal point Portland, Oregon.
2. Between the terminal point Reno, Nevada, the intermediate points Lake Tahoe and Sacramento, California, and (a) beyond Sacramento, the coterminal points San Francisco and Oakland, California, and (b) beyond Sacramento, the intermediate points Stockton, San Jose, Monterey/Salinas, Fresno, Bakersfield, San Luis Obispo/Paso Robles, Santa Maria, Santa Barbara, Oxnard/Ventura, and Palmdale/Lancaster, California, and (c) beyond Palmdale/Lancaster, the terminal point Las Vegas, Nevada, and (d) beyond Palmdale/Lancaster, the terminal point Inyokern, California, and (e) beyond Palmdale/Lancaster, the intermediate points Burbank, Los Angeles, and Long Beach, California, and the terminal point San Diego, California.
3. Between the coterminal points San Francisco and Oakland, California, the intermediate points Sacramento, Stockton, San Jose, Monterey/Salinas, Fresno, Bakersfield, San Luis Obispo/Paso Robles, Santa Maria, Santa Barbara, Oxnard/Ventura, and Palmdale/Lancaster, California, and beyond Palmdale/Lancaster, as in segment 2 above.
4. Between the terminal point Seattle, Washington, the intermediate points Tacoma, Olympia, and Aberdeen/Hoquiam, Washington, Astoria/Seaside, Portland, Albany/Corvallis, Eugene, Bend/Redmond, North Bend/Coos Bay, Roseburg, Medford, and Klamath Falls, Oregon, and Sacramento, California, and the coterminal Oakland and San Francisco, California.
5. Between the alternate terminal points Seattle, Washington, and Portland, Oregon, the intermediate points Tacoma, Yakima, Wenatchee, Ephrata/Moses Lake, Pasco/Kennewick/Richland, and Walla Walla, Washington, and Lewiston, Idaho/Clarkston, Washington, and (a) beyond Lewiston/Clarkston, the intermediate points Pullman, Washington/Moscow, Idaho, Spokane, Washington, and Kalispell, Montana, and the terminal point Great Falls, Montana, and (b) beyond Lewiston/Clarkston, the intermediate points Baker, Oregon, Ontario, Oregon/Payette, Idaho, Boise, Sun Valley/Hailey/Ketchum, Twin Falls, and Burley/Rupert, Idaho, and (c) beyond Burley/Rupert, the intermediate point Pocatello, Idaho, and the

EXHIBIT 11-1 Continued

terminal point Idaho Falls, Idaho, and (d) beyond Burley/Rupert, the terminal point Salt Lake City, Utah.

6. Between the terminal point Reno, Nevada, the intermediate points Las Vegas, Nevada, Grand Canyon, Kingman, Prescott, and Phoenix, Arizona, and the terminal point Tucson, Arizona.
7. Between the terminal point Tucson, Arizona, the intermediate points Phoenix and Yuma, Arizona, El Centro, San Diego, and Santa Ana/Laguna Beach, California, and the terminal point Los Angeles, California.
8. Between the terminal point Tucson, Arizona, the intermediate points Phoenix, Arizona, Blythe, Indio/Palm Springs and Riverside/Ontario, California, and the terminal point Los Angeles, California.
9. Between the terminal point Las Vegas, Nevada, the intermediate points Apply Valley and Riverside/Ontario, California, and (a) beyond Riverside/Ontario, the terminal point Los Angeles, California, and (b) beyond Riverside/Ontario, the terminal point Santa Ana/Laguna Beach, California.
10. Between the terminal point Tucson, Arizona, the intermediate points Phoenix, Prescott, Grand Canyon, and Page, Arizona, Las Vegas, Nevada, Cedar City, Utah, and the terminal point Salt Lake City, Utah.
11. Between the terminal point Tucson, Arizona, the intermediate point San Diego, California and the terminal point Los Angeles, California.
12. Between the terminal point Salt Lake City, Utah, and the terminal point Los Angeles, California.
13. Between the terminal point San Diego, California, the intermediate point Indio/Palm Springs, California, and the terminal point Las Vegas, Nevada.

International

1. Between the terminal point Spokane, Washington, and the terminal point Calgary, Alberta, Canada.
2. Between the coterminal points Phoenix and Tucson, Arizona, the intermediate points Guaymas, La Paz, and Mazatlan, Mexico, and the terminal point Puerto Vallarta, Mexico.

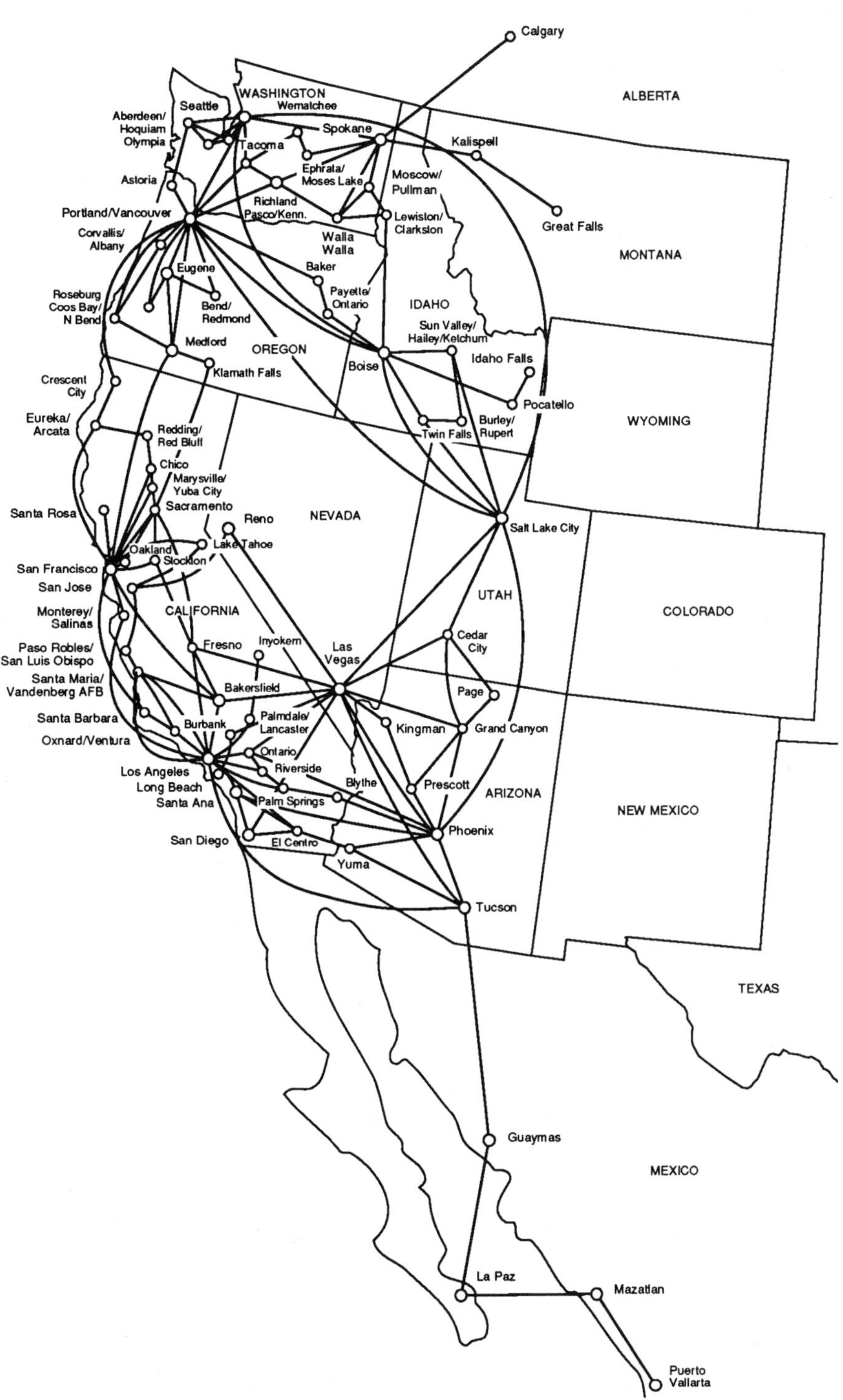
Calgary
ALBERTA
WASHINGTON
Wenatchee
Seattle
Aberdeen/
Hoquiam
Olympia
Spokane
Tacoma
Kalispell
Ephrata/
Moses Lake
Astoria
Moscow/
Pullman
Richland
Pasco/Kenn.
Portland/Vancouver
Lewiston/
Clarkston
Great Falls
Walla
Walla
Corvallis/
Albany
MONTANA
Eugene
Baker
Roseburg
Coos Bay/
N Bend
Bend/
Redmond
Payette/
Ontario
IDAHO
Sun Valley/
Hailey/Ketchum
Medford
OREGON
Boise
Idaho Falls
Klamath Falls
Crescent
City
Pocatello
Eureka/
Arcata
Burley/
Rupert
Twin Falls
WYOMING
Redding/
Red Bluff
Chico
Marysville/
Yuba City
Sacramento
Santa Rosa
Reno
NEVADA
Salt Lake City
Lake Tahoe
Oakland
Stockton
San Francisco
San Jose
UTAH
Monterey/
Salinas
CALIFORNIA
COLORADO
Cedar
City
Paso Robles/
San Luis Obispo
Fresno
Inyokern
Las
Vegas
Santa Maria/
Vandenberg AFB
Bakersfield
Page
Santa Barbara
Palmdale/
Lancaster
Burbank
Kingman
Grand Canyon
Oxnard/Ventura
Ontario
Los Angeles
Riverside
Long Beach
Blythe
Prescott
Santa Ana
ARIZONA
Palm Springs
NEW MEXICO
San Diego
Phoenix
El Centro
Yuma
Tucson
TEXAS
Guaymas
MEXICO
La Paz
Mazatlan
Puerto
Vallarta

Ground Properties and Equipment

Western Express general offices were located in leased space in the Fourth National Bank Building in San Mateo, California. Its principal maintenance facilities and training base were located at Sky Harbor Airport in Phoenix. The company had subsidiary maintenance facilities located in leased hangars and shops at San Francisco International Airport and at Boeing Field, Seattle. It also had approximately 31,000 square feet of floor space in an office building it owned in north Seattle. This office building was formerly used as the executive offices of West Aero Lines prior to its merger into Western Express. It was substantially unoccupied except for a small portion used for the reservations operations of WE in Seattle.

Western Express also maintained facilities on a lease basis throughout its system for sales, operations, cargo handling, communications and maintenance service, and downtown and airport ticket sales offices.

Western Express owned spare engines, other spare aircraft parts and miscellaneous ground property, including shop tools and equipment, ramp equipment, passenger equipment, ground communication equipment, automobiles and trucks, furniture and fixtures and underground fuel storage facilities located at various airports.

Competition

Western Express was subject to competition from surface carriers to all the points it served. Western Express was also in limited competition with major and other air carriers over large parts of its system. However, WE provided the only air service to 31 of the 83 airports it served. Western Express received no subsidy under the Essential Air Service provision of the Airline Deregulation Act.

Flight Equipment

Western Express placed orders for a total of 16 de Havilland Dash-8 turboprop aircraft. By February 1989, seven were on hand and the remaining nine were scheduled to be delivered between March and July, 1989. The capital expenditures forecast assumed that the aircraft would be leased.

There were 10 other Dash-8s on hand as of February 1989. Two of these were on lease from New England Airways until March 1989, at which time they were to be returned.

In addition to the Dash-8s, Western Express had eight DC-9-30 aircraft. Three of these had been leased to Superior Airways for a period of 52 weeks with option to renew.

Other aircraft in the combined inventory included 16 F-27A aircraft, 12 Beech King Airs, 9 de Havilland Twin Otters, 7 Cessna Caravans primarily used to carry cargo and mail, and 6 Piper Navajos.

Financial Condition

At the time of the merging of the three predecessor companies into Western Express, resources of the three carriers were already strained (see Exhibit 11-2). For example, there was a lack of adequate working capital, shown as follows:

Western Express Days of Working Capital as of June 30, 1988

Total Operating Expenses			Average Number
2nd Quarter 1968	Per Day (91 days)	Working Capital	of Days Working Capital
(000)	(000)	(000)	(000)
$17,232	$189	$(2,789)	(14.8)

Negotiations were under way to remedy this pressing need. A loan was entered into on July 31, 1988 with the Bank of United States providing for borrowing up to $54,000,000. Of this amount, $8,000,000 was allocated to refinancing short-term debt, for general purposes, and to write off $3,000,000 of deposits with the lending banks. Under this agreement, Western Express was required to maintain at least $1,000,000 of working capital, which would have been equal to approximately five days of operating expenses at the levels experienced during the second quarter of 1988.

This working capital level, even after the completion of the $54,000,000 loan, was less than half the average number of days of working capital available for other regional carriers of a similar size. The decrease in working capital, shown in Exhibit 11-3, was $1.7 million in the third quarter of 1988.

The lack of financial resources and strength resulted in severe constraints being placed on the operating officials of Western Express and in significant management problems for the merged companies.

On January 15, 1989, Western Express and Nationwide Air Holdings filed a statement with the DOT estimating the loss for the fourth quarter of 1988 at $4.4 million, based on the information then available.

Exhibit 11-3 contains summaries of defaults existing under various loan and lease agreements. These estimated amounts as of January 1, 1989 ranged from a low of $3.9 million under one provision of the Bank of United States loan agreement to a high of $20.5 million under another provision. The Federated Coastal Bank trust agreement covering the Debon Air Dash-8 leases showed a default of $13.1 million and the Seattle National Bank loan default was more than $15.6 million.

Western Express owed amounts to vendors and debtors other than the banks. By December 31, 1988 these were $3.5 million. More than $1.1 million of this amount was over three months old and $125,000 was over

EXHIBIT 11-2 Western Express Balance Sheets

	As of Dec. 31, 1987 (000) (1)	As of June 30, 1988 (000) (2)	As of Sept. 30, 1988 (000) (3)	As of Dec. 31, 1988 (000) (4)
Current assets	$ 15,436	$ 15,064	$ 17,181	$ 14,417
Property and equipment net (including prepayments)	50,702	60,058	67,469	66,564
Development and preoperating costs	2,985	4,478	6,334	6,655
Deferred financing costs/other assets	1,846	1,472	1,396	1,608
Total assets	70,969	81,072	92,380	89,242
Current liabilities	12,263	11,541	20,277	24,789
Long-term senior debt repayment due within 12 months	2,092	2,615	9,000	9,000
Long-term senior debt—banks	26,716	32,420	28,540	27,158
Long-term equipment deferred payments and notes	—	—	5,266	4,897
Long-term debt, subordinated notes	—	6,307	3,607	3,607
Subordinated debentures and other	9,244	8,861	8,559	8,000
deferred income taxes	1,223	702	702	702
Stockholders' equity:				
Retained earnings	5,777	4,575	2,082	(3,547)
Paid in capital & common stock	13,654	14,052	14,347	14,635
Total stockholders' equity	19,431	18,627	16,429	11,088
Total liabilities and net worth	70,969	81,072	92,380	89,242

EXHIBIT 11-3 Western Express Comparative Financial Indicators and Defaults under Various Agreements

	Dec. 31, 1987	*June 30, 1988*	*Sep. 30, 1988*	*Jan. 1, 1989*
Net working capital[1]	$ (831)	$ (658)	$ (2,346)	$ (8,622)
Net worth	$ (1,325)	$ (922)	$ (1,431)	$ (7,305)
Debt/net worth ratio[2]	$ 16,278	$ 7,093	$ (5,945)	$ (20,454)
Commensurate balances	—	—	$ (2,701)	$ (3,874)

Under Federated Coastal Bank Trust	
As of December 31, 1988:	($000)
12-month operating expenses less depreciation and amount	$ 68,114
Net working capital @ 8%	2,725
Estimated net working capital as of December 31, 1988	(10,372)
Default amount	($ 13,097)

Agreement Under Seattle National Bank Loan	
As of December 31, 1988:	(000)
Current liabilities	$ 24,789
less current payments due on loan	(750)
	$ 24,039
Required current assets at 1.25	30,049
Estimated current assets as of December 31, 1988	14,417
Default Amount	($ 15,632)

[1]As defined in Bank of United States Agreement.

[2]2:1 debt to net worth action required by Bank of United States Agreement used for all periods.

five months old.

Exhibit 11-4 shows the extremely critical financial condition of Western Express in February of 1989 as indicated by two letters from Western Express to Nationwide Air Holdings.

Problems Facing Western Express

The merger between the three regional/commuter carriers to form Western Express was brought about by the high capital needs of each of the three airlines. It became apparent that none of the carriers alone could have met the capital requirements for successful operation. The postmerger experience of Western Express was also plagued with problems. Financial problems were so acute that the only road appeared to be finding another financially strong company to acquire Western Express. In December 1988, top management from Allied Airlines held several meetings with officials of Western Express and their financial backers, but particulars could not be worked out. Finally, in mid-January 1989, Western Express filed an application with the DOT for approval of the acquisition of Western Express by Nationwide Air Holdings, a large finance and leasing group. Also in January 1989, Western Express retained a consulting firm to examine the problems of Western Express and make recommendations.

Two cause and effect views of the problems facing Western Express are contained in the following two summaries of conditions in Western Express after the merger.

CONSULTANTS' SUMMARY VIEW NO. 1

A single thread runs through the entire fabric of the problems of the merged Western Express and that is the management problem itself. It could easily be termed a struggle for control, but that greatly oversimplifies the problem. Essentially it is a conflict between philosophies and thus between methods of doing business. The control problem is a problem of *no control.* There is no singular direction; there is no unified management or control. There is no commonality or consensus of standards, values, or objectives. This fact is readily apparent to virtually every employee in the company and the very existence of the problem cannot help but have a seriously depressing and disruptive impact on the entire operation. If there is any one thing that is essential to curing this company's problems it is the absolute necessity of ending divided control, or no control, in fact. A unified management and control should be provided.

Keeping in mind the overriding management problem and its sweeping ramifications, if there is any other cause that could be identified as that underlying Western Express' current financial predicament and operating losses that cause would have to be identified as the com-

EXHIBIT 11-4

February 4, 1989

Nationwide Air Holdings, Inc.
P.O. Box 12345
San Francisco, CA 94000

Attn: Robert S. Smythe
Executive Vice President

Dear Mr. Smythe:

By this letter, Western Express, Inc. urgently requests immediate and maximum financial assistance from Nationwide Air Holdings, Inc.

Western Express's need for financial assistance is critical. Cash resources available, including cash generated by operations and other internal sources, are only sufficient to cover current requirements for a period of 10 days. These resources will not be sufficient to meet the payroll due February 14th. Despite repeated applications, we have been unable to obtain additional financing from the Bank of United States, our primary financing agency, or from any other source fo financing. The Bank of United States has informed us that it will not supply any further funds in the absence of a satisfactory participation by Nationwide Air Holdings.

Financial assistance by Nationwide Air Holdings is the only means of avoiding total disruption of Western Express services that will occur if the payroll and other pressing requirements for cash cannot be met.

Based on the latest available information, our present assessment of the current and prospective financial condition of WE, for the first three months of 1989, is a cash need of $6.7 million. The problems are even more serious than was conveyed in our earlier assessment in connection with the joint application for approval of the acquisition of Western Express that was filed with the Department of Transportation on January 17, 1989.

We now estimate that the losses experienced to date are substantially heavier than estimated earlier, totaling $10 million for the six-month period from August 1, 1988 through January 31, 1989. Our updated projection of cash flows through March 1989 show a deficiency of $6.7 million. We are in default of our loan agreement with the Bank of United States to the extent of $10.2 million at December 31. Unpaid and overdue vendor claims total $3.5 million at December 31 and have not yet been paid.

We estimate that the net losses experienced in January and projected for February and March 1989 on the basis of present trends will cause further defaults under the application provisions of the loan agreement with the Bank of United States to the extent of $9.9 million. We request the maximum assistance that may be given.

We are ready to provide you with any further information that may be required and we will give any assistance that we are able

EXHIBIT 11-4 Continued

in connection with application to the Department of Transportation for requisite approvals. We appeal to you to give this urgent matter your immediate attention.

Sincerely,

WESTERN EXPRESS, INC.

W. R. Donato
Vice President—Finance

* * *

February 5, 1989

Nationwide Air Holdings, Inc.
P.O. Box 12345
San Francisco, CA 94000

Attn: Robert S. Smythe
Executive Vice President

Dear Mr. Smythe:

This is in further reference to our letter of February 4, 1989, requesting financial assistance from Nationwide Air Holdings, Inc. to meet the now critical need of Western Express. In view of the urgency for funds, which it appears may now occur before February 14, referred to in our previous letter, and considering the time required by the need to have our attorneys file an application with the Department of Transportation to obtain their approval, we strongly urge and request an immediate meeting with you and your representatives to establish the amount of financial assistance you believe we have proven a need for and the terms under which you would be willing to render such financial assistance.

To avoid further delays and to enable you and your representatives to have further facts and figures prior to this meeting, we are attaching a schedule of WE's cash flow, which was not previously available for inclusion in our last letter.

Amount of Financial Assistance Being Requested

Western Express hereby formally requests the financial assistance of Nationwide Air Holdings in an amount not to exceed $6,683,000 to be disbursed to WE as needed by them for the continued operation of the airline through March 31, 1989. In our letter of February 4, we estimated that Western Express will incur cash expenditures that total $6,683,000 in excess of cash income in the first quarter of 1989. All the cash expenditures involved are set forth in the attachment and are considered by us to be essential to the continued operation of the business, with the possible exception of interest and aircraft leasing payments items totaling $1,696,000, which may be deferable if the forbearance of the banks and the de Havilland Company can be obtained.

EXHIBIT 11-4 Continued

Use of Proceeds

It is intended that all funds that may be advanced under a financing arrangement with WE be used by WE to discharge obligations incurred for the operation of the airline during the period from January 1 to March 31, 1989. Western Express does not intend to use any of these funds to pay any indebtedness incurred prior to December 31, 1988.

Methods of Funding

Western Express requests consideration be given to the following alternative methods of funding the financial assistance requested:

1. Arrangements with the Bank of United States for funding WE's cash requirements. Said funding to be guaranteed by Nationwide Air Holdings in a manner agreed on by the Bank of United States and Nationwide Air Holdings.

2. Direct funding by Nationwide Air Holdings to WE under an appropriate loan agreement.

Western Express intends to request funds under either method sought as they become necessary for the operation of the airline and is prepared to accompany all requests for funds with adequate evidence as may be agreed on to establish their need for said funds.

Financial assistance would be subordinated to indebtedness to Bank of United States.

Interest

We suggest that interest should apply at rates currently applicable to borrowings outstanding pursuant to the loan agreement between WE and the Bank of United States, dated July 31, 1988, unless more favorable terms can be arranged. That loan agreement provides for interest at 3/4 percent above prime, changing as the prime rate changes from time to time.

Repayment

Amounts obtained by Western Express under the financing assistance arrangement will mature on January 1, 1991.

Will you please wire when and where we may meet with you.

Sincerely,

WESTERN EXPRESS, INC.

W. R. Donato
Vice President—Finance

pany's extremely poor operations. This inferior performance has depressed traffic levels and therefore revenue far below what it should be under the merged operation. Not only has the merged operation with its resultant new services not generated new traffic to be added to the normal growth experienced by the separate carriers, but it is now actually producing results below the combined total of the separate carriers a year ago—with nearly 50% more capacity. While there is no way of determining with any degree of certainty the traffic volumes that WE should in fact be carrying today, it is our judgment that revenue level is a good million dollars or more a month less than what could have been reasonably expected.

In addition, the inferior quality of the operation has caused substantial cost increases that would not have been incurred in a smoothly functioning operation. Overtime cost, for example, has in recent months been running in excess of a quarter of a million dollars a month, some 2.3 times as much as that experienced in total by the three separate carriers in a comparable period before merger. Interrupted trip expense has been running at more than four times the combined total of the three separate carriers. In September and October of 1988 the total interrupted trip expense of approximately $175,000 was in excess of the total interrupted trip expense for the separate carriers for the entire year of 1987.

These two factors, overtime and interrupted trip expense, demonstrate somewhat dramatically the deterioration in the quality of the operation. Performance of schedules, on time or within 15 minutes of schedule, under the merged operation has been in the 40 percent range. This is vastly below anything experienced by any of the three separate carriers and obviously drastically below anything that could possibly be considered as an acceptable level of performance.

That the operation has been extremely poor by virtually any reasonable standard can scarcely be disputed. To turn the operation around, however, we must examine more closely the underlying causes for he failures. Dealing first with this problem on a more general basis, it can be said that the merger was somewhat unique and that it therefore presented unique problems. Normally in airline mergers one large company absorbs a much smaller company and the large company's operation is by virtue of the merger increased in size by perhaps 20 or 30 percent. In such a situation the rules, procedures, union contracts, practices, policies, philosophies and management of the large company generally dominate or prevail. Here three companies of somewhat equal size were merged with the resulting operation being at least 200 percent larger than that of any of the separate companies. Thus the monumental problem was melding, not imposing differing rules, procedures, contracts, practices, policies, philosophies and management under a partnership concept and agreement. In almost all cases the rules, procedures, and practices of any one of the constituent companies were totally inadequate for a company more than triple in size. Hence, new ones had to be devised or adopted and the training and learning process had to begin anew.

Concurrent with these problems there were massive movements in personnel and equipment to new locations and wholesale reassignments in personnel duties and responsibilities. Many personnel were lost and many new ones were hired to fill the vacancies. The personnel in WE's accounting department, for example, are roughly 60 percent new. During the intensive preparation for merger the management of each company also had to continue its own separate operations. In many instances one or more of the separate companies was also instituting new services and developing new route operations.

The magnitude and shape of the problems of the merged company were by no means fully anticipated. In consequence, on July 1 when the merged schedule was inaugurated, Western Express got off to a start that was almost disastrous, and this at the start of the peak traffic season of the year. Many things failed to mesh and a number failed to function properly. Adaptation to the new scope and concept of the operation was far short of adequate. The transition problems led to a level of efficiency far below anything that could be expected in a normal operation. The extremely bad performance that characterized the operation from the outset led to a terrible public image of Western Express. The result of this was that the traveling public avoided WE at almost any cost. If there was any other possible way to go or any way to avoid the need for travel if it had to be on WE, the public did so.

A number of these problems might well have been avoided or more successfully coped with had the merged company been in a stronger financial position at the outset. There was, however, a definite shortage of capital resources. At the time of the merger in the spring of 1988 the combined operation showed a substantial loss and there were indications that that loss would continue or perhaps mount for some indefinite period of time. Management knew that they would encounter costs that could not be fully anticipated. They knew that they would encounter a number of expenses, even though of a nonrecurring nature, that would aggravate the problem for some time. Conditions were not such as to permit any long-range financing decisions so only a short-term financing program was finally consummated, some three and a half months after the merger became legally effective. Had the company been in a strong financial position with abundant capital resources, that could well have had a significant influence on the character and quality of the company's planning. In the strained financial climate that existed, however, there was an overzealous effort to cut costs and produce, if possible, at least a small profit in the early stages of the merger. This was very likely the most costly course that could possibly have been pursued. It nevertheless appeared to be a driving necessity.

The biggest single identifiable problem in terms of completion and on-time performance of flight schedules was the inability of the maintenance department to support the operation. The aircraft simply were not available to maintain the schedules. Many were released late for commencement of the day's schedules; many simply were not able to complete the day's operation; and many suffered serious delays for maintenance requirements during the course of the day. There were of course delays and cancellations caused by a number of factors other than maintenance, but it was and is the dominant cause. It must also be said, however, that the department was also beset by the kind of problems that ran through the entire company, such as organizational problems, new assignments, new responsibilities, new faces, new procedures, strange equipment and so forth.

Other causes for delays in WE's schedules arose in the stations and in flight control, and many were caused by unrealistic flight leg times incorporated into the schedules. The station delays were attributable to new forms; gate congestion resulting from air traffic delays and plain off-schedule operations; and delays caused by new personnel, strange equipment, and slower ticketing. The latter resulted largely from new fares, new schedules, new cities and new markets. Roughly two-thirds of the system was unfamiliar to each of the agents.

Flight control, staffed by personnel from each of three carriers, was often working with aircraft, areas, airports, and weather conditions with which they were generally unfamiliar. It took more time. All three carriers operated F-27As, but each fleet differed in many respects. Each required special consideration. Two of the carriers operated Dash-8s, but these aircraft differed in many respects. One of the carriers operated DC-9s and no Beech King Airs.

Air traffic control delays have had an extremely adverse impact on the economics of the WE operation.

Cumulative delays were far more common on the WE system than they had ever been on any of the separate carriers. This stems from the fact that on the separate carriers' systems no given aircraft was scheduled over the extended geographic area of the WE system. In the case of the smaller operations opportunities for a make-up of time at nearby terminals or nearby turnaround points were much more readily available. Under the WE pattern an aircraft may well operate from one end of the system to the other and back again with few, if any, significant opportunities for make-up. The size of cumulative delay problems has necessitated schedule revisions that permit substantially more ground time for this purpose alone. This in turn has substantially lowered fleet utilization from that contemplated and significantly extended the total enroute time. In retrospect it probably would have been far better to continue the Dash-8 and F-27A operations somewhat in the manner operated by the separate carriers and effect the system route consolidation with the jet aircraft operating on the through services with their longer hops and fewer stops.

A great deal of trouble was encountered in the reservations department in the early stages of the operation. Much of this has since been cured. Here again, personnel from each of the three companies were working with new fares, with new cities and markets with which they were almost totally unfamiliar, and with wholly new flight numbers. Under the separate operations the carriers had maintained a good many of the same flight numbers over a period of years. These numbers were associated with particular markets and generally with a particular time frame. The new numbers, new cities, new markets, and new fares inevitably slowed considerably the time within which a reservation call could be handled. On top of this, the number of calls received by reservations after the merged schedule was published increased by a phenomenal 40 percent. Many of the calls were strictly for information purposes, for example, a call from the ex–Debon Air areas as to whether Western Express serves Baker, Oregon, or Walla Walla, Washington, and, if so, what it would cost from here to there and what kind of schedule was available. With questions of this nature, together with the requirement that nearly all answers required some searching, the time for handling a reservation call more than doubled. Western Express simply was not staffed for that increased and unanticipated workload. In response to that problem, training was intensified, more telephone lines were added, and additional personnel employed. Increased familiarity of personnel with the new route system likewise was helpful. Frequent schedule changes of course compounded the complexity of the problems for all personnel. These changes were made in part in an effort to help ease the operational problems and in part, particularly in later months, to help obtain a more productive operation.

During the entire period spanning preparation for the merger and the postmerger period to date, WE was taking delivery of new Dash-8 aircraft. During that period, seven Dash-8 aircraft have been delivered and integrated into the operation.

At the time of the merger, the three companies employed approximately 3,100 people. Western Express today employs more than 3,800. One hundred and thirty-six pilots were hired and trained in 1988. Additionally, 181 pilots that were with one of the three companies have had to be retrained and upgraded. The seat-mile capacity being operated today is 49 percent higher than that operated by the three carriers a year ago. The present level of operation would produce on an annual basis 58 percent more available seat miles than the carriers operated in calendar 1987. Traffic for January 1989 was approximately 217,000 passengers. A year ago, in January 1988, the three airlines combined carried approximately 221,000 passengers, or 4,000 more.

During the months immediately preceding the April 1988 merger approval and the five months immediately following that approval, Western Express or one of its constituent carriers inaugurated new routes and new services between Seattle/Portland and Salt Lake City, nonstop and via Boise; between Phoenix/Tucson and LaPaz, Mazatlan, and Puerto Vallarta in Mexico; between Tucson and Los Angeles, Tucson and Las Vegas, and Tucson and Salt Lake City; between Salt Lake City and Las Vegas, nonstop and via Cedar City; Salt Lake City and Los Angeles; Las Vegas and San Diego, nonstop and via Palm Springs; and provided some new services resulting from the combining of the three systems.

The computer, while no longer directly affecting the on-time performance of WE flights as it did in July, is not yet producing the basic data management must have to evaluate, direct, and control the operation of the company. These very basic management tools are woefully lacking thus far.

CONSULTANTS' SUMMARY VIEW NO. 2

Western Express's financial crisis stems principally from failure to meet passenger forecasts, failure to stay within predicted costs of operation, compounded by poor completion and on-time performance factors, adversely affecting revenue.

The seeds of WE's problems were sown when merger negotiations produced the costly requirement that Phoenix, Arizona be the maintenance base for the performance of all major check and overhaul work.

Upon merger, F-27A and Dash-8 aircraft, previously examined at a major base approximately every 3 days, suddenly were away from a point of major maintenance for periods of 8 to 28 days. These extended periods away from a major maintenance base caused most aircraft arriving in Phoenix for checks to have multiple deferred items to be performed along with those of a routine nature. Accordingly, checks could not be completed as scheduled, thereby producing inordinate numbers of flight cancellations, delays, and high overtime costs.

The initial merged schedule was deferred one month when flight operations found pilot training requirements were greater than originally anticipated and other departments, similarly, were unable to meet the requirement of the postmerger schedule. Further compounding the situation was the fact that jet schedules could not be flown on time, either because leg times were too short for distances involved, or because of increased times due to ATC congestion problems.

As in most airline operations, communication is the vital and binding link that makes it possible to meet public service commitments. At WE, a new computer system was implemented July 1, 1988, concurrent with the introduction of its first merged schedule. The new system completely replaced the original communication system. The installation was such that the older system was not available for backup, even though the new system had not been tested under full load for performance and reliability.

From inception, the new computer system was unreliable and troublesome. The software program, acquired from another carrier, was not thoroughly tested. When program problems occurred, there was no simple way of finding solutions. The system occasionally became totally inoperative for hours on end, leaving only telephonic communications available for systemwide communication. Messages were dispatched but never arrived. Full days of operational information were wiped out, unable to be retrieved except by weeks of painstakingly searching scattered records. Messages backed up on disk packs were unable to be retrieved or forwarded and were forever lost.

Investigation and solving of the software problem required many painful weeks. During this period, tremendous backlogs of data processing work accrued. Reassembling lost or distorted information was time consuming. When the software problem was resolved, it became apparent that the mechanical portion of the data processing system needed bolstering.

Additional lines were needed, crossover capability between lines, plus installation of emergency backup power. During the time of acquiring and installing the necessary equipment, shutdowns still plagued the communication system. Among many unfortunate results were the following:

1. Delay in consolidating programming and systems to replace the data processing operation for the former constituent airlines since all EDP staff were required to maintain operations and cure the problems of the communication system.
2. Timely dispatch of aircraft, communication of schedule delays, cancellations or maintenance problems remained unreliable through summer 1988.

Accurate flight time information was not available. Maintenance could not establish when checks were required on aircraft or when time items required removal.

To meet safety requirements, maintenance initiated a time padding system. Average daily aircraft time was supplemented by adding a 25 percent pad (that is, an average 8-hour aircraft day was recorded as a 10-hour day). Under this formula, aircraft checks and time component removals occurred substantially earlier than normal. The additional maintenance work included heavy overloads for overhaul and accessory shops, as well as premature and costly work by outside repair agencies. This additional work, falling during scheduled check periods, inevitably resulted in maintenance work taking longer than scheduled and contributed to high overtime costs and unforeseen delays and cancellations.

While all efforts were devoted to solving the switching problems, sparse statistical information was available. This impaired filing of DOT and other timely reports required by federal agencies. It delayed construction of a unitized payroll program and prevented production of all statistical operating information needed to evaluate the status of airline income, expenses, and performance.

Since the merger, labor problems existed. None resulted in work stoppages. However, Western Express has been involved continuously in negotiations with one or more of the unions on its property. Jurisdictional labor problems required representation elections to produce single bargaining entities for the flight attendants group (two unions involved), maintenance employees (three unions involved), agents, reservations, and clerical employees (three unions involved). This situation created costly diversion of the attention of employees from their normal functions.

Costs in excess of those forecast for the last three quarters of 1988 were as follows:

April 1 through June 30, 1988	$ 682,147
July 1 through September 30, 1988	2,793,037
October 1 through December 31, 1988	1,656,450
Total	$ 5,131,634

These amounts include the following categories of additional costs:

1. All home purchase plan costs.
2. All costs related to employee moves, that is, mileage, meals, furniture, and so on.
3. Salaries and wages of personnel in travel status at company expense.
4. Cost of furniture and inventories, that is, all company properties.
5. Flight training costs.
6. Cost of introductory and image advertising.
7. Cost of changing insignia on company properties, including painting aircraft.
8. Cost of new uniforms.
9. Fare revisions.
10. Outside consultant costs.
11. Severance pay for employees not moving.
12. Personnel hiring costs.
13. Personnel training costs (other than pilot).
14. Nonproductive man hours.
15. Personnel employed in excess of forecast.
16. Cost of living increase for transferees (the San Francisco area).

17. Excess maintenance costs due to premature checks and time component removal.
18. Excessive overtime.
19. Miscellaneous costs.

QUESTIONS

1. What is your diagnosis of the situation? What evidence supports your conclusions?
2. What recommendations and plan would you offer? Explain.
3. Describe the implementation of your plan and a timetable for action.

J.S. REYNOLDS COMMUNITY COLLEGE